The Golden Room

A Practical Guide for Death with Dignity

Innovative and Peaceful Solutions
For End of Life

By

Lynn Keegan and Carole Ann Drick

The award winning authors of
End of Life: Nursing Solutions for Death with Dignity

Some material in this book was adapted from Keegan, Lynn and Drick, Carole Ann (2011). *End of Life: Nursing Solutions for Death with Dignity.* New York City: Springer Publishers, Inc. Used with permission. For more information see: http://www.springerpub.com/product/9780826107596

Cover Design by Jon Quick absolutemaxpr.com

ISBN: 1481990373
ISBN-13: 978-1481990370

Library of Congress Control Number: 2013901187
CreateSpace Independent Publishing Platform
North Charleston, South Carolina

About the Authors

Lynn Keegan, RN, PhD, AHN-BC, FAAN is one of the founders of the holistic health focus in nursing and a past president of the American Holistic Nurses' Association. Lynn was elected as a Fellow of the American Academy of Nursing and is board certified as Advanced Holistic Nurse. After years as an educator she currently writes and consults. She has authored or co-authored 18 books and scores of professional journal publications and chapters in books. Dr. Keegan is a five-time recipient of the prestigious American Journal of Nursing Book of the Year Award and Distinguished Alumnus from Cornell University – New York Hospital School of Nursing. Her current focus is as an advocate for end of life ritual, placement and passing.

Carole Ann Drick, PhD, RN, TNS, TNSCP is an early and well known leader of the holistic health focus in nursing. She currently is President Elect of the American Holistic Nurses' Association. Carole Ann's holistic certification came through the International Fellowship of Introspection, Inc. receiving Teacher of Natural Science and Teacher of Natural Science Certifying Practitioner Certifications. She has authored or co-authored three books and numerous professional publications. Dr. Drick is a recognized speaker, author and consultant and two-time recipient of the prestigious American Journal of Nursing Book of the Year Award. She advocates for death with dignity, compassionate care and shifting the attitude around dying.

The Tree of Life

The Tree of Life resonates a simple yet
strong message of unity and living in harmony
with all human beings. This harmony at
the end of life is demonstrated through
dignity, goodness, compassion, peace and release.

Preface

Knowledge is comfort.

The more we know about the death and dying, the more comfortable we become. Knowing doesn't take the sting of loss and sadness away. Knowing does help us to prepare so everyone can move through death and dying with a higher degree of comfort and understanding.

This practical guide was written to do just that to give you comfort. It provides guidance and information so you can prepare for either your loved one's death or your own.

Death comes unbidden to all of us. For many it is one of the most difficult things to talk or think about. Our society has moved us away from the place of importance that death once held. Today death is a subject that is not part of normal conversation. It is not a happy thought; it is uncomfortable and scary to many. This book gives you the **opportunity** to explore the facts and understand the process of dying. It **guides you** as to what you can do to make the process smoother and easier. It **offers information** so you can make decisions based on knowledge rather than in the throes of emotions. This book **empowers you** to walk with death and dying knowing that you have value and worth that you are prepared and everything will fall into place in the most kind and gentle manner as possible.

This book introduces the idea of *Golden Rooms* where everyone can have death with dignity not just a select few. It introduces an idea whose time has come. The health care system is ready for innovative cost effective changes that enhance quality of life. *Golden Rooms* can deliver. We the people are ready for a shift back to individual worth and dignity. That makes this book relevant to everyone as we will all die. There are no exceptions. This book plants seeds of what could be – no – what SHOULD be. Death with dignity is everyone's right. This book is empowering to each who reads it and realizes that they can prepare for the inevitable. You are not powerless nor does fear have to immobilize you. You can take action now!

Knowledge also brings great comfort in the form of beginning conversations. This book is a conversation opener for family and friends. It provides basic ideas of what to expect and how to plan for rich golden year's right up to the end.

This book is a guide beyond the medical.
This is about life; death is a part of it.

Knowledge is comfort.
Golden Rooms are the answer.

Lynn Keegan, PhD, RN, AHN-BC, FAAN
Carole Ann Drick, PhD, RN, TNS, TNSCP
Find us at: www.GoldenRoomAdvocates.org

The Golden Room
A practical guide for death with dignity

Table of Contents

Part One
Consider the Facts

The Tree of Life

The Tree of life symbolizes both the mental realm and the emotional realm. The facts can stimulate deep inner emotional responses and the emotional can color the facts.

One

We are all going home

Let's begin quite simply and straight forward:
We need a place to die.
Golden Room Option

The world is full of new technology, innovations, and advancing digits and gadgets. What we need and don't have is a place to die. We have intensive care units, birthing rooms, dialysis units, surgical and medical wings, but our world lacks dedicated places for the end of life transition. Probably this is due to the fact that most people live in denial that they or their family member will actually come to this time. In the American culture most people deny end of life.

This book is about developing and using specially designed places for life's last transition. It is time that we have dedicated rooms that allow for peaceful, compassionate dying. We call these places Golden Rooms. Here, within existing acute care hospitals and new free standing buildings we can create healing spaces for life's end. No longer should we tolerate intensive, invasive care for those in the final throes of life. Instead we need special, unique rooms where compassionate, well trained staff

3

*offers the best in end of life care to those destined to leave this
world.*

*One may ask how Golden Rooms differ from hospice care.
The answer is that hospice's admission criteria is within the last
6 months of life, whereas Golden Room care specializes in the
last 3- 10 days of life as the body is imminently closing down.
As such the care is very sensitive mentally and emotionally to
the immediate needs of the dying and their family as well as
physical comfort care, pain medication and complimentary mo-
dalities to relax and release. There are no tests, treatments, other
medications or things that are used in traditional care that suggests recovery. Natural process is allowed to occur.*

We all know we will die

There are approximately 2.5 million deaths every year in the
United States. It is time that we, as individuals and as a society,
pay more attention to where, when, why, and how we prepare
for and deal with the end of life.

Intellectually, we all know that we will die. It's the emotional component that scares most people. In general we have
learned to deal with frightening emotions. Yet for many of
us, consciously or unconsciously, we are in denial as to any
fear around death. Actually, we use denial and other defense
mechanisms all the time to protect ourselves from real and
perceived threats. Unfortunately, denying attention to death
doesn't stop it. The fact of the matter is that all of us are headed in the same direction. At one time or another, in one way
or another, we will die. How we accept this fact and then

prepare for death often times makes the difference. We can go out with grace and dignity or, in the worst case scenario, kicking and screaming leaving a chaos in our wake. How do you want to go?

As we wake up and accept the emotional fact that we are all headed elsewhere, the better off we become. This place we are headed is known as many things and in many ways. Some call this destination the mysterious hereafter, heaven, the afterlife, being with God, nirvana, the great mystery or the great unknown.

Stop and ask yourself, will I die one day? And if you answer yes, how do you plan to deal with that fact?

With this guide, we trust you will find the explanations and have the opportunity to explore the facets of death and dying to help you cope with this final journey. There are many facts and ideas to discover and consider.

Are we consciousness or solely a physical being?

At the heart of the issue, perhaps the primary question to ask is: are we consciousness or solely a physical being? Of course, this is not a simple question; it has been debated and discussed by philosophers, theologians and scholars for millennia. The current trend of thinking, which we support through lived experience, is we are consciousness in a physical body. In reality we are both. There are times we are physical and use our physical brain to figure things out; there are other times we are consciousness and have access to all the knowledge in the universe. Put like that who wouldn't want to have all that knowledge? We all have experienced that there is something more than our physical body when we are in nature, watch a sunset or sun rise, have our breath taken away with exquisite music, a taste or beautiful words. Something "moves" within us and we "connect," if you will, to some intangible feeling beyond words. Finding the balance between the physical and consciousness assists us to successfully navigate on this earth.

How people die

Most people who die are old and sick. Certainly there are those taken in their youth or others in mid-life who die unexpectedly in accidents and injuries or even an early onset of a fatal disease. The vast majority of us, however, die at the end of our physical life cycle when the body can no longer remain in balance because of illness or old age.

As people age, many develop chronic diseases that plague them in later years. Conditions such as arthritis, aged joints, diabetes, unruly digestive systems, weaken muscular systems, and hypertension (high blood pressure) are a few of the physical irritants many people live with during their senior years. Generally, however, that's not what kills us. The leading causes of death are (in order of occurrence):

- Heart disease
- Cancer
- Stroke
- Chronic lower respiratory diseases
- Accidents

- Diabetes
- Alzheimer's disease
- Influenza and pneumonia
- Kidney diseases
- Septicemia (blood infections)

Notice that dying of old age or natural causes is not listed as a cause of death.

How most enter the health system

Let's begin by accepting the premise that most people die when they are old and/or sick. Given this scenario, let's consider the ultimate event. There are thousands, perhaps millions of old people in America who live at home. For now let's use the example of those living at home, not the other millions who reside in nursing homes.

Of those seniors who live alone at home, many of them wear some kind of medical band jewelry transmitter. The reason for this rather recent invention is to notify emergency personnel when medical help is needed. Generally the button on the band is pushed by the wearer when they fall and cannot get up, feel they are having a stroke or heart attack, or feel faint or dizzy. If they are not one of those with an alert band, it is usually a family member who is with them or finds them who dials 911 and asks for EMS (emergency medical service).

What happens when EMS is electronically summoned? As most of us know, within minutes an ambulance and fire truck arrive at the residence. There's lots of noise and excitement and neighbors gather to witness the show. Generally when one subscribes to this service, a key pad is placed on the front door. The EMS enters the required numbers on the key pad, gets the key, enters the dwelling, and rushes to render aid. So here's the issue, at this point in the life cycle, more often than not, when emergency aid and transport is provided it is at or near end of life. Since we don't have a system in place to deal with a natural end of life, the elderly person is transported to the emergency room (ER).

Do you know what happens in an emergency room? This is the place that is designed for lifesaving events to occur. The ER or ED (emergency department) is located as one of the most often used entry portals to the acute care hospital: a place where people go to be fixed, cured, and returned to normal functioning.

The dying person will follow one of two scenarios. If they are successfully revived from the fall, stroke, or heart attack, they most likely will be admitted to the intensive care unit (ICU). Depending on the severity of their condition they may die within the first 24 – 48 hours. If, however, they survive the ICU they will either be admitted to a general medical or surgical unit for further care. After that multi-day stay in the hospital then they will either be discharged home, to a rehabilitation center, or to a nursing home. Some miraculously recover and go on to live a few more months or years. Many others are sent to nursing homes. It is here that they live out their remaining time. It is these institutions that have become the final home to most of American's dying senior population.

How we got here

In the early years of North America the country was largely composed of farming, extended families. Most folks were self-reliant and by living in rural areas they frequently witnessed births and deaths of farm animals. Thus death was an expected, and for the most part, a natural event. Families were large and everyone knew someone who had recently died or was dying. There were farm or industrial accidents, bouts of diseases such as typhoid and yellow fever, childhood diseases such as measles, whooping cough and diphtheria that resulted in numerous child death and flu epidemics. In the days before antibiotics, pneumonia was known as the old person's friend since that was the way many people passed on. Sulfa was the first antibiotic drug and came into use in the 1930s; penicillin evolved in 1943. Before the mid-20th century, most of the ill and dying received only palliative/comfort care at home.

During the second half of the 20th century technology boomed. Then everything changed. There were many new medical discoveries and health care inventions. Sick and terminally ill people fled from the comfort care of yesterday into the arms of the fully equipped intensive care unit. The era of the natural death was ushered out the door just like hanging laundry on a line in the yard. The automatic dryer and the intensive care hospital replaced the old ways. In only a few decades the whole way and feeling around death and dying had changed. The farming era dissolved into the industrial period and then into technological dominance. It was then that most of the extended family living close by dissolved. Driven by where the jobs were, families moved apart and the social fabric of family support and a strong sense of individual self-reliance crumbled. By the end of the century the predominance of older people, kept alive much longer by innovative medical intervention, now spent the remainder of their days in nursing homes. The irony is that these new havens for the older and disabled did not look good if their residents died in-house. So, what happened when they became gravely ill?

What happened then is exactly what is still happening now in the 21st century. An ambulance is summoned and the frail and frightened old person is transferred to the acute care facility. Here, faced with the life support tubes and gadgets, ventilators, IVs, and feeding tubes, many patients recover and are eventually returned to the nursing home. Those that die in the hospital are discretely removed (sent to the morgue). The fact that it might be natural to die is not in the picture. A passing via a natural death has been erased from the consciousness of the American psyche.

Today, some 50 + years later we are finally coming to grips with the fact that we have too many seniors and dying persons squeezed into too few end of life facilities with inadequate environment, trained staff and personal features. Too many of us are rushed to acute care settings, or find ourselves or our loved ones on the other end of the spectrum, alone in one of the thousands of nursing homes. These are some of the issues that we as a society and culture must address.

For the purpose of this little book we are taking a look at the individual and what each of us can do to enhance the quality of our lives at end of life. When we work on our own life we begin to affect those around us and, in this way, begin to change society.

Where do you want to spend you last days?
Probably the first thing we want to address is where we spend our last days. Most of us would like to know that there are options when that emergency occurs. Most of all EMS, doctors, nurses, social workers, and hospital personnel need to know that there are other options to the scenario above. Not everyone who has an end of life emergency wants or needs to be admitted to an acute care setting and the chaos that often ensues. It is when we individually and collectively pre-think the options that more opportunities and content endings are likely. To that effect we have more later on those topics.

Face the facts
And those facts are that we are all going to die. Now to use the word die to some will feel uncomfortable. That is not our intention. Rather our intention is to have you begin to become comfortable with the word and use the word in your everyday conversation. The fact remains that eventually every one of us, 100 per cent of us, will die. That's the heart of what we must come to grips with and prepare for. Begin to consider:

- Where you want to be at end of life?
- How do you hope your life will end?

- Who do you want with you at end of life?
- What do you want to happen after you pass on?
- What can you do to better plan for your death now?
- Are you ready to go?

These can be challenging questions to ask; and you, the reader, may tend to rapidly read over them or think "I'll look at these later." This is the tell-tale sign of being scared and denying. If this is the case, the question to ask is, "if not now, then when?"

Death with dignity
The greatest human freedom is to live and die according to one's own desires and beliefs. The most common desire among those with a terminal illness is to die with some measure of dignity. From advance directives to physician-assisted dying, death with dignity is a goal for all. Each of us needs to learn all that we can about this period so as to be able to make our own end-of-life care decisions.

The meaning of death with dignity
Death with dignity means different things to different people. Essentially it means concluding this physical life with composure, peace, compassion, in the way that has meaning to you. What all of us want is to know that we are in a place that someone cares for us and that we are kept comfortable and pain free. That is the essence of death with dignity.

Population projections
Based on current projections, the Nation's population is projected to increase to 392 million by 2050 – more than a 50 percent increase from the 1990 population size. These figures will also dramatically boost the number of senior citizens.

And we are getting older
About 30 percent of the population in 1994 was born during the Baby Boom, 1946 – 1965. People born during the Baby Boomer years were between 36 and 54 years old at the turn of the century (2000). In 2011, the first Baby Boomers turned 65; while the last of the Boomer's will reach age 65 in the year 2030. By then, nearly one in five U.S. residents is expected to be 65 and older. This age group is projected to increase to 88.5 million in 2050, more than doubling the number in 2008 (38.7 million). Similarly, the 85 and older population is expected to more than triple, from 5.4 million in 2008 to 19 million by 2050.

The US Census Bureau tells us that the mean life expectancy is projected to increase from 76.0 years in 1993 to 82.6 years in 2050. In 2050, life expectancy will range from 75.3 years to 87.5 years.

Beginning to take responsibility where we can
Today we are faced with seeming dire predictions coming from all directions with required action that needs to happen yesterday. Where do we begin and how? There are many things that we cannot do anything about such as our personal

aging and death, but there are also very many things that we can do. There are things that we can change such as:

- the care and quality of our dying experience
- letting others know what we want and what we don't want
- considering, developing and writing an action plan
- knowing who we want with us and where we want to be

We are entering a time of great change on all levels similar to the yin and yang symbol that suggests a duality of opportunities. On the one side is doing nothing, being fearful, stagnant and feeling helpless. This is allowing things to happen to us instead of through us. On the other side is the opportunity to take bold new, out of the box, steps to begin changing what is not working. Each heart felt step, large or small, is a step in solutions. What we all need is an alternative to enhance the quality of the death experience.

So ask yourself, is there some small step you can take now to move forward toward facing death? Are there questions you may want to ask yourself? Try the following to get started:

- What do I imagine and see when I reflect on the idea that someday I too will die?
- Does the thought of death frighten me? What emotion does it stir within in me?
- What can I do to befriend death so that I am not afraid anymore?

- Who can I confide in who will assist me to face death?
- How can I build or strengthen my spiritual base?
- What help or guidance do I need in this area?

The fact is that anything we can do to lessen our fears and face the fact that life does end will help us when the time of transition actually arrives. Each step along the way makes death, when it does come, easier and in many cases a kinder friend rather than an enemy to combat and resist. Remember and recall the tenants of living each day as our last:

- Be in this moment
- Acknowledge your feelings to your self
- Allow yourself to feel the feelings without becoming the feelings
- Observe the inner shifting in your feelings as you listen, talk and move through today
- Laugh a lot
- Tell others you love them
- Freely give and receive hugs
- Wake in the morning eager to see what this day brings
- Sleep in peace
- Repeat often through the day, "I sleep in peace, awake in joy and live in the expectation of good."

In summary, we are all going to die. How we prepare for this event will make the difference between dying with dignity and grace or other not so nice consequences. Read on to discover more specific steps and tactics you personally can take to create a more comfortable and informed journey to your final destination. And, begin to think about a new place for end of life care, a place called the *Golden Room.*

Two

The necessary details from A to Z

Golden Room Option
On the horizon

Golden Rooms are another possible site for your dying process that are just now coming on the horizon of health care reform. These are dedicated rooms much like birthing rooms where you could go for the last 7 to 10 days of life. These rooms will have dedicated staff specially trained to assist you and your loved ones to gently and gracefully walk together in your final hours of physical life. The surrounding will be calming with specially selected colors, pictures on the walls and ceiling, amenities for your family and comfort care for you. Pain medication will be available as needed. Gone are the tests and procedures and in their place is a recognition and feeling of allowing this natural dying process to take place. The attitude of the staff will be one of deep respect and sacredness at this time in your life.

These rooms are in the very early talking stages of development. The early ones will serve as examples for other hospitals and organizations to follow. Within our grandchildren's *generation the thought can be "How did we ever live without Golden Rooms?"*

A more complete description is available in our book, *End of Life: Nursing Solutions for Death with Dignity.* Our website www.GoldenRoomAdvocates.org also gives a clear portrayal of *The Golden Rooms.*

Think about the time you will die. Slowly now, take a deep breath and really consider that one day you will be gone. . . . . . Do you want your loved ones to scramble to figure out what to do? Imagine how they might feel. Suddenly or gradually, in one way or another, you are simply not there anymore. Consider how they will feel. Consider how you might feel looking down on them from the above. What would you want to be happening? Now think about what you might do to make the process easier for them. Do you want to? Would doing so give you or your remaining loved ones comfort?

End of life conversations
A good time to begin a dialogue with your loved ones is well before the fact that you will actually need them. The reality is that most of us do begin to lose some mental acuity earlier than you may realize. One study on financial decision making, called "Age of Reason" put the mental sweet spot – knowledge plus agility – at an average age of (gulp) 53. Of course, some of us stay sharp well into their 90's, on the other hand, many of us being the decline without even realizing that it is happening, or before we have our house and affairs in order. Where are you on the scale? Are you ready to start the dialogue?

Once you have done some thinking on your own, it is a good idea to begin talking with trusted others. For some it is not too difficult, but for many of us, this is a tough conversation to initiate. Sometimes it begins with a single statement such as, "I certainly wouldn't want what happened to Aunt Myrtle to happen to me." Your spouse/child/relative or other loved one might reply, "Well what happened to her?" From this unassuming example, you can see how a conversation about your wants and desires could begin. On the other hand, some people prefer a more formal end of life discussion and ask for their significant others to sit down and formally talk about it. Whatever method you use just know that it is a good idea and serves to get everybody on the same page and at the very least know that you are aware of the situation and have proactively chosen to discuss them. Then keep your family updated on your progress and ask for their inputs and ideas in the process.

Developing a plan – What it is and what it contains

It is wise to have some form of written communication. Some call it a plan, others a set of instructions, or some other name. Basically this plan is a set of instructions that tells the executer or first responder who to contact, what you would like them to do, and where valuables are located. This vital bit of information clarifies details of what to do in case of an emergency or after a person's passing. It makes the job of the executer of the estate or the first responder much, much easier to handle. There are lots of model plans; here is one example of a Plan that's a conglomerate of many others.

MODEL PLAN

Emergency Phone Numbers:
- Patrol or Association office of retirement village, condo association, or other pertinent offices
- Primary contact person/care giver and their phone number/address to come and help

Personal contacts to notify:
- List of all children: list name, their relationship, i.e. daughter, address, phone numbers, and email addresses
- List relatives with same locator data as above
- Friends with same locator data as above
- Community, apartment, condo, or neighborhood association office if relevant
- Employees, i.e. home health providers or business associates

Business contacts:
- Personal attorney
- Home and automobile insurance companies
- Business partners or place of employment (if relevant)

Health and medical records:
- Where to look for health cards, social security cards, etc. in your billfold or purse. Describe the location.
- Name of primary clinic and/or physician and their locator data

- Name and location of pharmacy
- Name and location of hospital for emergency room if needed
- Name and locator data for home health caregivers, hospice, delivery people, etc.

Final arrangement preferences:
List here if there are other or additional details not specified in the will. For example, you might write, "look in my bill-fold located in my purse in the bottom dresser drawer in the second bedroom for my medical insurance card information", etc...

In addition, you may want to write about how you would like your funeral to proceed and your preferences as to be buried and how. For example, do you want a traditional burial or cremation? Do you have a prepaid plan? Are there certain hymns or verses you wish to be read?

Data for death certificate:
Write specific information you would like for this form. You will need your date and place of birth, social security number, parents names, education level for yourself as well as your spouse.

Financial records:
Location of investment accounts, i.e. Brokerage Houses, banks, etc. For example, are they in a bank safe deposit box

or in a file cabinet or safe located somewhere in the home or apartment? If so, describe the whereabouts.

Location of Wills, Trusts, Power of Attorney, etc.:
Name and address of the banks and locations of the safe deposit boxes. List the names and account on the bank accounts and safe deposit box number.

What I/we owe:
- Itemize accounts and account number of items due: car payments, mortgage payments, taxes due and to whom payment is sent.
- Or write a statement such as: No mortgage, no car loans, no debts other than current monthly bills. You might state that all credit cards are paid in full on a monthly basis when received.

What I/we own:
- List bank accounts, credit cards, credit unions, and vehicles: account number, address, and phone number
- C.D.'s – same data as above
- Treasury Direct – Bills & Notes – same data as above
- Home deed certificate – location
- Automobiles
- List collections, antique furniture, oriental rugs, and other items of value

Accounts receivable:
List who owes you money, state their name, locator information and amount due and for what purpose

Investment accounts:
Give name of various accounts, account numbers, and locator information

Life insurance policies:
List names of policies and where they are located

Real estate:
List home address and any other property owned, i.e. rental property

Our/my monthly income:
- Detail monthly income sources
- Pension plan with employee number deposited to account number at which bank on which day of each month for the amount of $$$
- Social Security income and frequency. Give same details as in example above.

Other automatic income:
- List Dividends & Capital Gains and if they are reinvested.
- Interest earned, etc.

Main expenses:
Quarterly income tax payments, payable to IRS on April 15, June 15, September 15 of current year, and January 15 of next year or this year's estimated taxes. List utilities or other accounts such as community or condo association dues that are billed electronically or automatically to credit cards each month or quarter. Describe property taxes that are customarily billed in the fall and are payable at the city or county tax office. List location.

Additional information:
- Personal home phone number
- Personal cell phone number and access or passwords
- Personal email accounts and passwords
- Yard and household maintenance information: when they generally come and their locator information

In summary, the information contained in your Plan provides a vital tool to assist a family member or loving friend who is there to help during the dying process or after death has occurred. This tool helps make for an easy, much smoother transition than would happen without it. Take some time now and consider making your own roadmap to guide and aid those who will be there after you die.

Valuable legal documents
Never underestimate the value of a few good legal documents to ease the efforts of leaving this physical form,

especially for your heirs. There are a variety of tools to guide those who will follow you after death. These include, but are not limited to:

Power of Attorney (POA):

Giving someone the Power of Attorney allows them to speak on your behalf should you become unable to do so. Your POA pays bills, does banking, helps with medical, insurance, and benefits paper work. Without a power of attorney and if and when you become incapacitated, your relative or interested party must begin legal proceedings to be appointed as guardian. It is a formal document that needs to be witnessed. Do realize that this is a powerful document so think carefully and talk it over with the designee before you execute the paper work.

Advance Directives:

Advanced directives allow the individual to determine in advance their desires for end of life care. Although the statutes from state to state vary, advanced directives are a step in the right direction. As such they are an excellent place for individuals to state their preference for their choice for end of life care.

Living Will:

In years past an advance directive form was only used to express your wishes regarding healthcare decisions when you are permanently unconscious or have a terminal illness. Currently there is another form, the living will. This instrument appoints another person in advance to act as your healthcare agent if you become incapacitated. It provides instructions for others to make medical care decisions for you when you are no longer able to make them for yourself. A healthcare agent, sometimes called a health care proxy, patient advocate, surrogate, or health care representative, may also be appointed in advance to make these healthcare choices and decisions when you are not able to make them for yourself.

Some families have endured complicated and divisive end-of-life decisions regarding both beginning and removing life support systems. By making a living will, you may possibly save your loved ones both expense and emotional trauma. By taking the time in advance to express your preferences for medical care and life support, you can ensure that your loved ones will not be burdened with making difficult medical decisions on their own or through the courts. Living wills may be prepared with or without an attorney.

Will or Last Testament:
A will is a legal document that declares your last wishes. To whom to give what and how they are to receive the proceeds. It may be done with or without an attorney. If you avoid making a will you may leave numerous legal problems and disputes for your survivors after your death. When you make a will, you help ensure your belongings won't wind up in the wrong hands. Without a will your heirs may pay big extra costs, legal fees, taxes, and additional expenses. A last will & testament can also make sure other final wishes are carried out, such as funeral instructions, burial or cremation wishes.

Guardianship:

If you don't have a POA and you become completely incapacitated the court will appoint a guardian. Guardianship proceedings cost thousands of dollars. By creating a durable power of
attorney before incapacity, a guardianship or conservatorship
proceeding can typically be avoided and the agent can usually
act as a representative for you.

Trusts and estates:

A living trust is an effective estate planning tool for many individuals and is recognized as the best way to avoid probate.
A trust is a method of holding property in a fiduciary relationship for the benefit of the named beneficiaries. The same
individual may be the grantor, trustee and beneficiary. The
grantor may also name successor trustee if the original trustee
dies or is unable to serve, as well as successor beneficiaries.

To create a living trust, the owners of the trust (also called the
grantors or settlors) make a living trust document and transfer
real property or other assets to the trust. Assets are transferred
into the trust belong to the trust and are managed by the trustee. The trustee manages the trust property for the benefit of the
beneficiaries, according to the terms of the trust document

There are two basic categories of living trusts:

- A **revocable trust** which may be changed or terminated
  by the grantor (this is you) of the trust. The settlor
  reserves the right to take back any trust property and
  remaining revenues. What this means is that although

your funds and accounts are legally in the trust name, YOU (the grantor) still own and control your own money. Revocable trusts are also referred to as grantor trusts, and therefore the income is taxable to the grantor (you) and any assets in the trust when the grantor (you) dies become part of the grantors' taxable estate.

- An **irrevocable trust** is somewhat different. The difference is that this trust can't be changed or terminated without the consent of the beneficiaries. By transferring assets into the trust, the creator of the trust (you) gives up control and ownership. Therefore, the assets and income are no longer taxable to the grantor (you), nor do they become part of the settlor's taxable estate when he or she dies. Some types of irrevocable trusts include an irrevocable life insurance trust, irrevocable family trust, Medical income trust, special needs trust, and charitable trust.

Living trusts can provide many benefits, such as:

- avoiding probate,
- protecting assets from creditors,
- keeping your financial affairs confidential, or
- minimizing taxes, delay, and legal expenses.

When your estate is distributed under a will (after you die), you lose control over what happens to it once received by the heirs. Living trusts provide a way to protect and manage your estate even after your death or incapacity. Even with small estates, trusts can serve many purposes, such as:

- ensuring that your pets are cared for according to your instructions to the trustees,
- protecting government benefits or eligibility for Medicaid, or
- allowing you to maintain confidentiality in your financial affairs and choice of beneficiaries.

Then there are other, more complicated trusts. These include Bypass Trusts, Charitable Remainder Trusts, and other types. In the case of all trusts it is advisable to work with an attorney to develop any one of these documents.

In summary, initiating conversations about end of life and creating the right documents, rightly executed and carefully stored will give you important tools to facilitate a graceful closure and help foster a death with dignity. Take a look at your own documents and inventory what you have and what you may still need. Make a "to do" list and get going. If you need help in this department, now is the time to ask for it. Your heirs will be so grateful.

Three

What it costs to die

Golden Room Option
Let's cut to the chase

One way to dramatically reduce costs would be to have dedicated spaces, Golden Rooms, readily available in all acute care hospitals. When terminally ill, most patients are hospitalized. Their care becomes acute care, often times with expensive diagnostic tests, sometimes with surgery. Most caregivers realize this is futile care, but at the same time they placidly accept the acute care setting culture, death is not an option. Thus, at the same time expensive fees are created, compassionate end of life care in an appropriate setting is either denied or a last ditch hurry and transfer as death is imminent decision. As a culture we need to design and activate end of life rooms.

The population of the United States is rapidly aging. By 2030, the number of Americans aged 65 and older will more than double to 71 million older Americans. These older adults will comprise roughly 20 percent of the U.S. population.

In some states, fully a quarter of the population will be age 65 and older. Additionally, there will be 19 million people age 85 and over. These ages are advancing at the same time that inflation is causing prices of goods and services to explode upward.

With aging, more disabilities and more chronic diseases can occur. To add to the equation, the costs for end of life care are increasing exponentially and will continue to do so in the decades to come. For most of us we are waking up to the need for serious consideration of these financial costs at end of life. For example, we all know how diagnostic imaging is being used more and more. What we now are learning is that the use occurs even in people with end stage, advanced cancers. According to the Journal the National Cancer Institute, the use of diagnostic scanning is zealous with an average of 9.7 scans per patient despite their limited survival times. What we want to ask ourselves is, do we want or need all this expensive care at end or life, or would we rather spend the resources on peaceful and compassionate care and care givers in a holistic, comfortable setting?

One day all of us will outlive our physical body. There are no exceptions. The more we know and prepare for this final eventuality the better. By facing death proactively we can both come to peace with our physical mortality and lay the groundwork for our own end of life expenses.

Are we individually and collectively financially ready?

More than half of all workers or their spouses have less than $25,000 in household savings and investments. Since women still earn less than men and have a longer life expectancy, they are at greater economic risk. When women end up older and alone, whether it's widowed, divorced or never married, they have a fairly high rate of poverty. According to some sources, on average, about 20 percent of elderly women fall into the poverty category. Many others save and plan for retirement and end of life costs, but are faced with the inflationary recession that has rendered their savings inept to cover their needs. Some turn to their children for help, but unfortunately, not everyone has family, wants to or can live with them. According to AARP, 22.3 percent of women and 12.5 percent of men age 50-plus live alone. Another source of cost concerns are the 5.4 million adults with Alzheimer's. Up to half of these people have no identifiable caregiver. Thus the expense of their care falls on the government programs, Medicare and Medicaid.

End of life care costs
The cost of caring for seniors is a growing major concern. Providing health care for an older American is three to five times greater than the cost for someone younger than 65. By 2030, the nation's health care spending is projected to increase by 25% due to aging Americans. Shifting the attitude and consciousness around death and dying from fear and life at any cost to dignified caring for each dying person would certainly make a difference in the end of life costs. This is beginning to

be recognized within health care with discussions on how to address this growing need.

Costs of dwellings

Toward the end of life we have choices of where to be. Many factors are involved in choosing where your dying experience should take place. When we talk about costs most of us immediately consider financial costs. There are also emotional costs, resources, and caregivers to name a few. Here are a few of the physical locations with some of the associated costs to consider.

Independent living facilities

These are group housing and group homes where some people live. These are independently organized and may or may not be licensed. This independent housing is generally the least expensive way to live, but usually lack being overseen by a government or health care agency nor do they offer any health care on site.

Assisted living facilities

Assisted living facilities are located where many people reside, but they are neither cheap, nor are they end of life facilities. Since many elders live there, we will mention them.

Some of these complexes require a rather large "deposit" which you may or may not get back. This differs markedly from one facility to another.

In assisted living generally you care for yourself, but many facilities do have a nurse on call and a restaurant where meals are served. One caveat about most assisted living facilities is that most require that in an emergency you be able to get from your bed and out an exit door in 12 minutes or less – by yourself. If you, for example, need assistance in transferring from you bed to a wheel chair, you may not meet the requirements for living there. When you are no longer able to completely care for yourself, generally you are transferred to a nursing home or a wing within the living complex if the skilled care option is located in the same geographic area.

Assisted living facilities do offer some assistance in your activities or daily care needs. Many have 24 hour staff nurses for all medication management and room checks as needed. MetLife Mature Market Institute, 2011 Market Survey of Long-Term Care Costs data found that annual costs run about $41,724 per person for assisted living care. Some agencies, however, may cost up to $100,000 per person per year.

Nursing homes

Nursing homes offer skilled nursing care when you are no longer able to care for yourself or when your family can no longer care for you. They also offer around the clock staff, call bells for help, immediate medication for pain relief, and resources to keep you clean and comfortable. Unfortunately nursing homes are already bulging at the seams with residents and a fairly high turnover of staff and often minimum staffing.

U.S. nursing homes are approved to accept Medicare, Medicaid or both. The cost of nursing home care is typically higher than assisted living, and this is where it gets really pricy. Check in your area. In many locations the price will range between $4,000 to $7,000 per month or $48,000 to $84,000 a year. The average cost of a nursing home care is more than $67,000 a year and tops $100,000 in some urban areas. These costs generally do not include pharmacy bills, barber or beauty shop expenses, foot care, dressings and treatments, and many other miscellaneous therapies and supplies. MetLife Mature Market Institute, 2011 Market Survey of Long-Term Care Costs data found that in 2011 the mean cost was $87,235 for a private room in a nursing home.

The average nursing home patient runs out of money within six months and must go on Medicaid. If this trend goes on unchecked not only will it bankrupt individuals but also the Medicaid system.

Have you priced end of life care options lately? As you see above, the prices will astound you. Call around in your area just to get a sampling. Take a tour. Ask questions about staff: patient ratios, and turnover and facility certification. Gather your data in advance to know what you are signing up for before making your decisions.

Swelling numbers of elderly end up in nursing homes. And as it turns out, the majority of nursing home services are funded by the Medicare and Medicaid programs. Medicare long term care services are covered by Part A, "Skilled Nursing Facility" (SNF) services which are associated with post-operative or post-hospitalization including rehabilitation therapies. However, when post-hospitalization coverage runs out, generally after three months (90 days), private or personal pay kicks in. The other coverage by Medicaid (paid for by the state) "Nursing Facility" (NF) services is provided to state residents who meet the Medicaid eligibility requirements.

Per capita nursing home spending on the frail elderly aged eighty-five and over is OVER TWENTY TIMES HIGHER than spending on the young elderly, aged sixty-five to sixty-nine. The number of these frail elderly is expected to triple or quadruple as America ages. Now and in the recent past many families have qualified their elderly parents for Medicaid through subterfuge: transferring the elders' assets to their children. Congress is actively moving to close that loophole. The final sad statistic is that almost two-thirds of people in nursing homes have no living relatives, and about 70% of all nursing home patients are women.

Hospice

Hospice is a great resource and one that makes fiscal sense. There are, however, still some issues with hospice. Although popular opinion is that hospice is for imminent dying, referrals are accepted if death is expected within six months. Even this can be extended as long as there is declining health. One can enter hospice at any point in the dying process with an order from the physician. Usually the entrance into hospice is at the very end of life when death is imminent. Hospice can be either at a specific location or in the home. In order for hospice to be in the home, there must a primary care taker in the home either family or friends. The hospice nurse is like a visiting nurse and does not stay with the dying person rather makes frequent visits and supports the family/care givers in the dying process. Check to see if hospice care is available in your community, the requirements for admission, what it includes and, of course, the financial impact to you.

The financial cost of hospice care has continued to escalate along with the rest of the economy. Most importantly since many families do not entirely understand the hospice end of life care concept they call for emergency help when they become scared. Once admitted to the hospital for acute care treatment frequently hospice usually does not accept them back into their program.

Home care

For the vast majority of people when you ask where they want to die, they will say that they want to die at home. This is a lovely comforting vision yet many questions remain of which two are most pertinent: At what cost? Who will be the care givers and do they have the physical stamina and ability to give the needed care? Consider the cost of having round the clock care in-home at say a hypothetical fee of $18/hour which is probably low. For this fee the person would be a NA or certified nursing assistant ($8-10/hour average) or higher needing a supervisory level. The RN would do interim visits and treatments. This adds up to $432 a day, $3,024 a week, or $12,096 a month. Think of the supplies and gadgets that are often not added into the equations, for example adult diapers, special food supplementation, sterile supplies and monitoring systems. These miscellaneous items can cost up to hundreds of dollars a month. Always there is other specialized equipment needs such as safety bars, special beds and sheets. Unless there is a way for insurance to help pay for in home care, it becomes prohibitively expensive for most people.

The advantages of the home setting are multiple:

- One is less agitated and more peaceful in familiar surroundings
- A familiar setting helps you to remain focused and less confused.
- The caregivers are family who are also comfortable in the setting.

All the costs and benefits must be taken into account to bring the best possible care to both the dying person and their family.

Considering Resources

The nation's current economic crisis makes addressing health care issues even more urgent. With health care spending on track to reach 50 percent of America's GDP by 2050 and states in severe budgetary straits, cutting waste and creating new and innovative improvements to achieve savings and create better care is an imperative. Incremental change isn't enough. With the oldest of the 78 million boomers turning 85 in 2031, the government tab alone could be staggering. In 2021, Medicare alone is expected to cost taxpayers $1.1 trillion — up from $586 billion in 2012.

Population demographics indicate that birth rates will fall and life spans will continue to lengthen over the next two decades, driving up the median ages in many countries. The U.S. is now passing through an important demographic transition. Public discussion about the impact of this transition focuses primarily on how the aging population and, in particular, the imminent retirement of the sizable baby boomer generation, will lower national savings. This discussion often ignores additional important and potent demographic forces, including

- the behavioral differences in savings patterns between baby boomers and subsequent generations,
- the reduction in the birth rate,
- and the impact of the demographic transition already underway in many of the world's most important economies.

In the past, aging of the baby boomers supported wealth accumulation as they moved through their peak income and saving years. Now the strong behavioral trend is to save less. As baby boomers enter retirement with fewer savings many may encounter significant financial challenges. As Boomers save less, younger generations will also save less, and birth rates will slow. The resulting decline in the growth rate of financial wealth accumulation means there will be less household savings to support a fast-growing retiree and indigent population. At the same time, it will become increasingly difficult to support domestic investment and sustain economic growth.

End of Days

According to new research published in the Archives of Internal Medicine, health care costs at the end of life show no signs of leveling off. Americans spend about a third of our overall health care resources in the last year of life.

Often it is in the last couple of weeks of life that costs spiral out of control. For many whose families have not planned for their last days they follow a typical pattern. An emergency happens and they call 911. From there they generally are admitted to an acute care hospital via the emergency department. Without specific preplanning the scenario escalates to treating their terminal or semi-terminal condition as an acute care condition. As a result of this redirection of dying as an acute care condition, medical and surgical interventions are ordered with the costs quickly adding up to hundreds of thousands of dollars. This is called spending on futile care. Denial and fear of litigation by most hospital practitioners results in attempts to cure the patients in their final stages of life. As a result huge sums are spent on a futile cause.

It is here in these last weeks or days that expenses can wipe out personal saving accounts and insurance reimbursements. It is here at this stage we need to rethink how we are rendering care to offer the best service at end of life. Should it be with invasive, expensive care in a hospital, or rather should it be in dedicated, caring, end of life rooms staffed with experienced staff who understands the end of life process?

It is now that you need to investigate your options and your family options. It is now that you need to talk about what is financially feasible and begin to make provisions for this eventuality. To be informed and make intelligent decisions rather than emotional quick decisions is one of the differences that make for a peaceful death. It is your life. You get to choose. Choose wisely.

Part Two
You have Options

The Tree of Live

The Tree of Life represents
all the choices that you have to make
plus the deep inner foundation of
truth and wisdom that can lead your choices.

Four

Where to be at end of days

Golden Room Option
A *new* concept in hospice

A Golden Room or Rooms is a new concept that builds upon and furthers the idea of hospice. "Golden Rooms" or "Golden Room Centers" are special places for those within 7 to 10 days of dying. Golden Rooms can exist in nursing homes, assisted living centers, hospitals, and in free-standing dedicated end-of-life centers for the last days of life. Central to Golden Rooms is a shift in the way we view death. Rather than a tragedy to be avoided at all costs, death is accepted as inevitable for us all and a meaningful release of the spirit from the physical world. Please refer to Chaper 5: The Golden Room for a more complete description.

Take a few moments to consider where you want to be at end of life. Are you comfortable at home – for now? Maybe you are not living at home now; perhaps you are in an assisted living facility or community group home. Do you like the setting where you are? Do you think you may want to remain there? What if you become incapacitated or near death?

Do you know the options? Have you carefully weighed them? Have you consulted your loved ones or a close friend? Have you discussed these matters with your attorney, family counselor, parish priest, clergy, or pastor? Are there some places to be at end of life that you may not yet know about?

Considering the choices, places to spend your final days
There are quite a few choices these days of where to be at end of life. For the purposes of this book, we are talking about end of life, not simply elder care in one's senior years. There are lots of options for your elder years, but end of life is generally considered to be within the last six months or last few days. The places you may choose include:

- Assisted living facility
- Staying at home
- with family or living alone
- at home with home health agency help
- Palliative care
- Hospice – in a center or at home care
- Golden Room(s)
- Nursing home
- Acute care facility

Assisted living facility
Assisted living emerged in the 1990s as a form of senior care for individuals who could no longer live on their own, but did not require 24-hour supervision or assistance provided by

nursing homes. These facilities traditionally provide custodial-care services in group settings. Residents in assisted living can get assistance with bathing, eating and dressing, and many facilities offer shared meals, housekeeping and laundry services and group activities. The thing to know is that assisted living facilities are not licensed or regulated on a national basis, but on a state-by-state level. Assisted living care fits into a spectrum of definitions, with facilities called assisted living homes, personal care homes, and residential care homes. Of primary importance is the fact that these facilities work until the time to die. If one resides there when death is imminent, then they are generally transferred to an acute care setting or nursing home.

Staying at home

With family or living alone
This setting use to be where most people stayed. In the old days, most people had extended families and there was generally some relative available to tend to the old one who eventually died at home. Those days, however, are mostly gone. Extended families have morphed into smaller nuclear families. Many live in blended families with children from more than one marriage, others live in a variety of different ways. Today there are many now single people who have divorced and no longer have a spouse to care for them in times of need. Still other old people survive their spouse, who has already passed on, and are now alone. True, some of these remaining, now single elderly, move in with their children, however,

many do not. Lots of widowed and divorced people live solo in apartments, condominiums, rooming houses, senior living communities, or assisted living facilities. This is well and good – until they begin to die. Many of these dwellings are not suited for end of life and thus, other arrangements need to be made. The good news is that there are lots of choices.

At home with home health agency help

If you are among the group that has family to live with, you have choices of which and what type of agency or kind of private care. There are a number of both national and local home health agencies that cater to the shut in and needy individuals. These agencies provide a full range of service by various levels of prepared caregivers including:

- Registered nurses who administer services such as intravenous medications, breathing machines, and other devices to assist with comfort and care
- Trained and certified home health aides who monitor blood pressure, test for diabetes, assist with administering pills, and do basic level of physical care
- Home health aides who help organize the house, bathe, and do personal hygiene
- Helpers who can grocery shop, cook, and do rudimentary house keeping
- Companions who can sit and read to you or simply keep you company

Receiving assistance in your home setting for a variety of services and functions is the simple definition of in-home care. The advantages of using an in-home health agency include:

- The agency handles the hiring of the caregiver and the related paperwork and taxes.
- Most home care agencies provide a back-up caregiver if the standard caregiver is sick or on vacation.
- Home care agencies can send professional caregivers to provide skilled care, such as nursing care or physical therapy.

On the other hand, like everything else in life, there are also some disadvantages:

- You may not be able to choose the caregiver that is sent to the home to assist your elder.
- Home care agencies are typically more expensive than private caregivers.
- An agency may not send out the same caregiver each time, which could affect the continuity of care.

For those who have the means there are many free-lance individuals who provide care. They offer the same services as an agency, but may not necessarily be state certified. The advantage of hiring a private individual or team is that you may be better able to control the hours of care as well as negotiate the pay. Remember that when hiring a private person it is fee for service and no state or federal social service agency will pay. On the other hand, unless you are on Medicaid or in a special provision of Medicare or have some specialized insurance policy, you are responsible for paying all of the home health agencies.

Palliative care

For the past several decades, a number of options to ease the dying experience have emerged. Medical treatment, once primarily focused on acute care, has expanded to include palliative care and hospice care. The goal of palliative care is to achieve an optimal quality of life for patients by using a holistic approach that focuses on the alleviation of pain, symptoms, and other unique needs of the patient at any time during their experience with a serious or life-threatening illness. A combination of social support, emotional support, and attention to spiritual aspects of care and respect for the patient's culture, beliefs, and values are essential components of this approach. Although the level of palliative care intensifies at the end of life, the focus on the relief of suffering and improvement of quality of life is important throughout the course of the illness, and aspects of palliative care can be provided along with life prolonging treatment during earlier phases of a patient's illness.

Hospice

Hospice care is an organized program for delivering palliative care that involves an interdisciplinary team of specially trained health professionals and volunteers. Hospice care may be delivered to dying patients in inpatient units, nursing homes, or, most often, in their own homes. In addition to providing palliative care and personal support to individuals at the end of their lives, hospice provides support to the family while their loved one is dying as well as during the bereavement period. In 1982, Medicare began reimbursing for hospice services. To qualify for the Medicare hospice benefit, terminally-ill patients must have a terminal diagnosis, a life-expectancy of six months or less, and is willing to forgo further treatments. Patients who live longer than six months can be "recertified" if their situation still meets the criteria for the hospice benefit.

Nursing home
Nursing homes, sometimes referred to as skilled nursing facilities, provide continual, 24-hour medical attention to their residents. For seniors who have significant medical problems, severe cognitive issues or mobility impairments, nursing homes are equipped to provide the proper level of care.

Some facts about nursing homes include:

- There are some 16,100 homes in the USA
- There are approximately 2 million beds
- There are 1.8 million residents
- The occupancy rate is 86%
- The average stay is 835 days (remember there are 365 days in a year)

Many elderly people spend their last days in nursing homes. However, due to the exploding expansion of home health care only about 7.4% of Americans aged 75 and older lived there in 2006, compared with 8.1% in 2000 and 10.2% in 1990.

Since there are so many single people or those with whom a family can no longer care for, millions of us eventually end up in nursing homes. Initially these facilities were designed as a bridge between the acute care hospital and the return home. A period of recuperation and rehabilitation was spent here. Our society has evolved from an extended family in a chiefly rural setting to nuclear families in large urban areas. Nursing homes have become the place for folks when they can no longer fend for themselves and have nowhere else to go.

According to the American Association of Homes and Services for the Aging's Institute for the Future of Aging Services, approximately 25% of all deaths occur in nursing homes. Despite this, less than 20%, fewer than one in five nursing homes, offer end-of-life programs. So consider where do you want to be?

Acute care setting

For many the acute care hospital is the place where they die. As we saw in Chapter 1, the majority of people or their relatives, not knowing any better alternative, panic in the final days or hours, and call 911 or in some other fashion get themselves to a hospital. Generally, it's the emergency room. From there, since naturally in distress, they are admitted to either to the intensive care unit or a general medical floor. Here they are attended to by personnel skilled in acute care, not personnel necessarily skilled or even interested in dying care. And believe us, there is a huge difference. Some people get lucky and have caring staff that render comfort care and allow them to die with peace and dignity.

Far too often, however, medical, surgical and nursing staffs aren't geared to losing their patients and thus, do all they can to keep them alive. This is where, when, how and why acute care setting deaths are not the destination of choice. Acute care is just that – acute. That generally means using life support machines and therapeutic techniques, including surgery, to keep people alive. If and when individuals and our collective society accept the fact that dying is a natural part of the life cycle, that we are more spirit than physical beings, then we will choose not to use acute care settings for end of life care. There are so many other more desirable options. Is it your time to explore them?

EOL care decision making

Family members are often asked to make decisions on behalf of a loved one who is seriously ill without having a complete understanding of his or her preferences. To avoid this situation, you would definitely benefit from discussing end-of-life wishes with family members and health care providers well before the onset of a serious illness, and designate a surrogate decision maker for health care as discussed in Chapter 3. Having these conversations is the best way to protect one's independence in a myriad of unpredictable situations.

Gathering company (who do you want with you?)

If you have not here-to-fore thought about whom you would like with you at end of life, this is the time. Maybe there is a friend or family member who could come and be with you at end of days. Reflect now and perhaps even initiate a conversation to let them know you would like them to be by your side as you part this world. Consider how you might make this happen. You might buy them a plane ticket to travel to you? Might you tell them of your wish for them? Are there some final gifts that you could make to them? If you do not have relatives or close friends maybe you might reflect and offer some of your belongings to neighbors or service clubs or a charity. You might even consider one or more of your caregivers.

Saying goodbyes'

Saying good byes can take many forms. Often distance is a challenge especially as we age. You might make a telephone call and have a long delicious chat about all your good times together and how much they have meant to you over the years. Good byes also can be a time of saying "I'm sorry" or "let's let all this go and remember the good times." Sometimes a letter or card can be in order – this can go both ways.

For many with more advanced technology, using the computer program Skype, face to face Internet communication or even a smart phone, substitutes well for being together in the same physical space. Skype and some smart phones enable both living video stream and voice connections. They work well to bring family into each other's person in home space.

Above all consider a good time and place to say your final goodbyes. It's true that many people will remain in denial until close to the end. Remember that it's never too late to be finally ready. Do it now while it's on your mind.

In summary, there are a variety of nesting places at end of life. Today there are more choices than ever: home with family, home with health care agency aid, hospice, Golden Rooms, nursing home, and the acute care setting. Some of these settings have more advantages than others. Consider them all and think about where you want to be. Read on to learn the specifics about the option of *The Golden Room*.

Five

The Golden Room

The Golden Room Option
The concept described

W e all would like to think that when everyone dies they will be surrounded by family usually at home with hospice care. Sadly this is not the case. More than half of the elderly die in nursing homes or in acute care setting and often alone. It is time to change what really happens and begin to extend quality of life to include the end of life.

The *Golden Room* offers a beautiful experience that surrounds the dying person and family with the comfort and dignity that the end of life transition was meant to have. Within this unique setting there is a depth of caring that can transform fears and concerns into a natural gentler passage. *Golden Rooms* are seen as a replacement to the impersonal acute care environment that is often filled with loud machinery, invasive tubes and rushing personnel.

As stated in Chapter 4: A *Golden Room* or Rooms is a new concept that builds upon and furthers the idea of hospice. "*Golden Rooms*" or "*Golden Room Centers*" are special places for those within 3 to 10 days of dying. *Golden Rooms* can exist in nursing homes, assisted living centers, hospitals, and in free-standing dedicated end-of-life centers. Central to *Golden Rooms* is a shift in the way we view death. Rather than a tragedy to be avoided at all costs, death is accepted as inevitable for us all and a meaningful release of the spirit from the physical world.

Golden Rooms specialize in the last week or two of dying as the body is imminently closing down. The care is very sensitive to immediate mental and emotional needs as well as physical comfort care. Without tests or treatments that suggest recovery, natural process is allowed to compassionately occur. By contrast hospice offers care and entry into their program during the six months of life. *Golden Room* care has the focus on the last days of life.

Nurses who work in this setting are chosen for their personality traits as well as their skills. They have been fully inserviced and comfortable with their own mortality. With such an orientation they give care from a place of an open love filled heart. Nurses in this setting also offer holistic techniques that assist in relaxation and feelings of well-being.

The Space

Imagine a space specially created for the end of life transition. Imagine *The Golden Room* as a physical place filled with feelings of rest and gentle being. All the colors, fabrics, and décor reflect gentle peace, relaxation, insight and rest. A full picture, wall mounted TV screen with images of gentle, sea creatures undulating through blue/green, foamy sea water replaces the

customary blaring TV sound so common in most patient settings. The pictures gently change every few minutes into a host
of birds and butterflies in various stages of gliding through
meadows then into fluffy, ever-changing, cloud formations
and nature scenes.

The walls are a lovely color and covered with washable,
sound absorbent material. On one side of the room is a bed with
an over the bed tray table. The supplies are stored in a bedside
stand giving the feeling of a more cozy bedroom. The windows
are clothed in versatile damask drapes opening to full day light
or closing with complete light blocking. This allows whatever
amount of natural light or darkness is desired.

The ceiling is designed with a tray style insert. Along the
four edges an 8 – 12 inch rim is dropped down to create a lovely
framing effect. Many contemporary bedrooms and some dining
rooms use this style. Within this framed-in area of the ceiling
there is a gentle, calming mural. The dying person has a full view
of the painted scene as it is just above and beyond their bed. In
Golden Rooms murals may be one of several forms reflecting the
universe. Some rooms might have pastel cloud formations, others a dark blue background with bright starts pebbled throughout an expanse of space or other appropriate murals.

The floor is a wood laminate. This gives the feeling of
warmth while allowing for through and easy daily cleaning.

Soothing music adds to *The Golden Rooms'* quiet and calming atmosphere. The music selections act as a natural pace maker
to slow the heart rate, brain waves and respirations of the patient
as well as their visitors. As such it assists the dying person to

release the physical body during the final hours before death by augmenting peace, recognition, and calm expectation.

Family comfort is taken into consideration. Another bed and reclining chair are available in a corner of the room. It is partitioned away from the hospital bed with sliding, moveable screens. This corner can accommodate two loved ones who desire to stay during the transition process. A roomy bathroom serves both the patient and the family.

Even the bedding is tailor made for *The Golden Room*. A different fabric is used rather than the familiar white, cotton sheets of general hospitals and nursing homes. Soft flannel sheets or thick thread count quality sheets cover the bed and invite greater comfort and ease. Fitted bottom sheets offer superior comfort and better shielding from the often crinkly noise and creases of the still necessary moisture protector mattress pad. A favorite blanket from home or comforter tops the bedding.

Designed for a homier feel the soft, comfortable furniture offers choice and reflects a feel of snuggling in and being at ease. The dimmer switch for the overhead lighting makes for easy, family directed control lighting. A side table lamp offers the option of adding additional colors of blues and purples, tones designed to relax and calm. The air may or not have the gentle aroma of essential oils as the person desires. They simply need to ask staff to initiate this additional element. All these comfort choices offer increased options to quiet the environment and create a gentle blend of calming options specifically for this person and their family.

Additional comfort techniques

Golden Rooms offer a full complement of comfort techniques that are available to the person and their family. Although there is an extensive list of offerings the types of comfort techniques can include: massage, aromatherapy, music, acupuncture, visualization, meditation, therapeutic touch and healing touch to name a few.

Pain management

Conventional pharmaceutical pain management is available to keep the person comfortable should they need it. Care is given to administer enough pharmaceutical medications to control pain but not an amount that would depress the patient's respiratory or neurological functions. Since many prefer their IV be removed, medications are generally delivered by the nurse via the intact port-a-cath or by mouth. On occasion the person may have an IV patient-controlled analgesia pump so they can control their own level and amount of pain medication. Many people have found that the complementary comfort techniques enhance their well being and pain medication is less often needed or in lesser amounts.

Allow natural process

Basic to *Golden Rooms* is allowing the natural process of the body as it actively closes down. Honoring the body's innate intelligence rather than interfering and "trying to support" the body to remain in balance is a delicate and loving process. What we see as the body out of balance is really the body in balance as it gently withdraws more and more first from its outer surrounding and interactions then gradually withdrawing from the more non essential then the essential body functions. This is a very gentle and exquisite process that has its own balance far beyond what man could ever develop. To be able to support and observe this sacred time is not only a great honor, it is often life changing for those involved.

Psychological and spiritual support
Psychological and spiritual support for both the person and their family is also available on an ongoing basis. This is through not only the traditional religious organizations but also through the holistic health care professionals in attendance who understand and honor religious traditions that may be different from their own. Chaplains, priests, rabbis, and/or the minister or pastor counselor of choice are available to both the person and the family. This pastoral care offers spiritual comfort, words of peace, and gentle release from the mind's worries about one's life, accomplishments, relationship and mortality. Others without a traditional religious faith may find comfort with an esoteric spiritual advisor, colleague, or readings.

Criteria for admission
Admission into the *Golden Room* is uncomplicated.

1. The person is within 3 to 10 days of dying.
2. The person/family is open to *Golden Rooms* and accepts "allow natural process."

3. The physician writes the order for the *Golden Room*.
4. The papers are signed.
5. The transfer occurs.

The health care professionals
Specially certified health care professionals, comfortable with their own mortality and with the process of death and dying, assist in creating the spiritual atmosphere of *The Golden Room*. Being comfortable with their own mortality is foundational to their success in assisting others in this natural end of life process. With this foundation they can be fully present for the person and their family at this most important last phase of life. As certified *Golden Room* care givers they have enhanced abilities to create close warm relationships with each patient and family. This can only result in a calmer more loving end of life transition for everyone present.

Setting the spiritual atmosphere
The purpose of the *Golden Room* is to facilitate and honor the dying process for the person and their loved ones. Thus all elements of the design must be taken into consideration and have been described. A sense of spirit is reflected in all the carefully chosen features of the space, the health care professionals and the additional comfort techniques. Together all these set the spiritual tone of the space and hold the presence of calmness and gentle process. It is this ambiance that enhances the experience for each and every person whether consciously or unconsciously.

Present availability
Presently, *Golden Rooms* are still in the creation process. Although they should be everywhere, they are not. For *Golden Rooms* to become a reality both the shift in consciousness and the first prototypes must be promoted. These places will be created when we awaken the social need and public demand to build them. All of us can write to legislators to change laws to create a less litigious environment at end of life. Many can band together and lobby organizations, hospitals, and political groups to include *Golden Rooms* in end of life care.

The first *Golden Rooms* and their locations are being discussed by health care professionals and hospital/organizations. Although still on the drawing board the level of interest has been exceptional as the need for them becomes more apparent.

Refer to the website www.GoldenRoomAdvocates to sign up to receive intermittent updates on our progress.

Advantages to *Golden Rooms*
The advantages to *Golden Rooms* are numerous and far reaching.

- *Golden Rooms* are dedicated to the imminent end of life; there are no distractions in the form of other types of palliative care as the care is specific to end of life.
- These rooms become the model for the most advanced and creative forms of physical atmosphere and

creative comfort measures for both the dying and their families.
- The entire staff is specially trained and concerned with the person, family and their situation.
- Acute care settings, nursing homes and physicians no longer have to be concerned with and fear litigation with increasing mortality statistics.
- *Golden Rooms* become a prized commodity both for death with dignity and for a hospital statistic representing caring rather than cold mortality.
- *Golden Rooms* are an inexpensive solution to rising costs for medical insurance.
- The humanity of death with dignity would return with *Golden Rooms*.

Within a generation the feeling would be,

**"How did we ever manage without
Golden Rooms?"**

Part Three
Death itself

The Tree of Life

The Tree of Life stands for
your physical "seen" life and
your spiritual "unseen" or inner
life which richly and continuously
connect together to give us mortality
and immortality simultaneously.

Six

How the body closes down:
What is natural and what to expect

Golden Room Option
Trained Staff to love and support you

As you read about the body closing down, imagine a place where the nursing staff are specially trained to assist in this natural process of the body closing down with calm, loving support for the dying person and their family. Specially trained professionals can gently and compassionately guide the dying person and their family every step of the way. As a result a more gentle dignified release is made possible.

Although end of life comes to all of us, it is rare that this major life event is fully appreciated or understood by the majority of people. The body is specially designed so its systems close down through a sequential slowing down and eventually stopping with the heart's last beat. What we want to remember is that this closing down is a normal, natural process. Once we better understand this natural process the fear of what is happening is greatly reduced and we are able to better receive comfort, compassion and care as the body

69

performs its final task of closing down. The better we understand this natural progression, the less upsetting and alarming it is as we experience death our self or support a loved one's dying process.

We are all going to die

Death can be a painful reality. Even so, it is the least understood body process because of three important facts. First, there is an emotional response to death on the part of the dying person and their family and/or loved ones. Second, each person and their family have a spiritual meaning attached to death and the dying process. Finally, death is the ultimate unknown and can only be entered alone. The simplest definition of death is a moment in time at the end of physical life which is preceded by a dying process.

The dying process

The dying process is a personal journey that usually begins well before physical death of the body. No one knows for sure the date and time of their death. Some have "feelings" that death is near but no one really knows. As one ages and the body slowing down becomes more noticeable, there is a tendency to progressively think more and more about death. The body slowing down or taking a longer time to heal is evidence of the beginning of the dying process though most people would disagree as this fact is hard to accept. Most people do not share these thoughts with each other or their family. When disease is part of the dying process, consciously or unconsciously, most people consider their imminent death and have some manner of preparation including watchful waiting. Even not preparing is a preparation!

The physical process of the body closing down
The body closing down is simply, logical and sequential. Once understood death can become less demanding and problematic making it easier to experience though the irreversible finality can still be distressing to some. Death comes when all the bodily systems cease to function. This normal, sequential, unromantic process is NOT a medical emergency that requires intervention; rather, this is the time to give love, compassion and comfort measures.

As death comes nearer
The body has an amazing ability to cope and adjust to all types of disruptions and imbalances. At first it treats the slowing down of different systems by adjusting, for example: breathing becomes more rapid to offset the decreasing power of the heart to pump blood to all areas of the body.

There are five primary systems that have major observable changes as death draws near:

- The <u>digestive</u> system slows with decreasing in appetite and results in weight loss.
- Diarrhea and/or constipation may be present as well as nausea and/or vomiting. The mouth can even have sores that do not heal.

- Changes in the <u>skin</u> are quite noticeable as the color pales to grey or even jaundice (yellowed). Loose skin from weight loss can be dry or irritated and pressure sores can arise quickly as there is skin on bones with no padding.
- As the <u>circulatory</u> system begins to fail the arms, legs and lower back may begin to retain water and sometimes the belly becomes swollen with fluid.
- Within the <u>urinary</u> system there may be incontinence, retention and/or infections with foul smelling, concentrated often cloudy urine.
- Most obvious in the <u>muscle and skeleton</u> system is the loss of muscle mass, tiredness and weakness.

Signs of changes usually begin slowly and appear over time, often many years before death. Signs vary greatly between people and are dependent on multiple factors including diet, sleep patterns, hydration, exercise, and mental attitude.

Mental, social and psychological changes
The dying person's approach to life and interacting with others has observable changes. There is a decrease in outer activities and more of a focus inward. Interest in family matters wanes and often there can be restlessness. There is an increased concern on being comfortable and in a safe place with their needs being met by others. Often there is increasing stillness and being quiet with disengagement from television, music or social plans and/or activities. With deepening awareness, gentle

acceptance and understanding of the process, more people are discovering that dying can be a time of active participation in the process. They desire to be awake and aware, comfortable and to live life to its fullest up to the last breath.

The last days
As the body closes down it begins to withdraw its energy from the extremities and focuses on the core of the body. There are many observable changes that occur. With the advancing signs of impending death, it soon becomes clear that the person has may be a couple of weeks to live. There are many normal changes in these last days as the body closes down beginning in the extremities and slowly progressing to the heart. Once familiar with these changes comfort measures may be introduced with the end result of supporting the body's process and not mistakenly hindering what the body so beautifully knows what to do: close down.

The first systems to close down are the digestive and elimination systems. As the body prepares for death the anal sphincter muscles relax often with a generous release of its contents. The urine becomes concentrates, "tea" colored and diminished in amount with decreasing fluid intake plus decreasing circulation through the kidneys. The neurological system begins to misfire resulting in twitching in the legs, arms and fingers. If holding a loved one's hand, this misfiring is often misinterpreted as a communication from the loved one. As the heart begins to struggle to pump there can be swelling in the legs and in the lungs. The body sometimes begins to shake.

73

Holding and gently rocking the person is a comfort measure for both the dying person and the loved ones.

Appetite and dehydration
Appetite is certainly one of the most common concerns of family and friends. The fear of starving the dying person is not reality; it is based on knowing how we feel when we have not eaten for a while or have been sick. Dying is a different situation: the body is closing down. The stomach has reduced digestive enzymes and ability to digest or assimilated foods/liquids. The gag reflex is decreasing and swallowing becomes more difficult. As a result, feeding tubes offer no change in quality or quantity of life. AND, once inserted feeding tubes are often difficult to have removed. Because of the irritation on the back of the throat, feeding tubes can even result in a more painful death. This is no longer the preferred method of nutritional support. Physicians now put in a G-tube that creates an opening directly to the stomach. Either way, the body is still closing down and food is not needed.

In the last hours of dying, dehydration appears to stimulate the release of natural pain killers called endorphins plus other anesthetic compounds that support a feeling of well-being. In the last days the person often refuses food and liquids as the digestive system continues closing down. This is a normal process that can be supported by simply moistening the lips. The body at end of life is conserving the energy of digestion to be used in supporting other more vital systems. In refusing food the person is not starving or rejecting loved ones and their offerings; it is the body closing down.

About this time intravenous fluids (IVs) are often considered or are already in place. Care needs to be given here since IVs can be supportive of some symptoms, yet this body is closing down in a normal natural way. The excess fluid that the body can no longer handle since it is closing down can result in a fluid overload. This in turn may cause both painful edema (swelling) and shortness of breath.

Wakefulness and sleep
As death approaches more time is spent in sleep and less time awake. Progressively more time will be in a sleep like state with increasing difficulty in being aroused. This is partly due to decreasing metabolism. This is a natural preparation for the transition and is neither a "giving up" nor rejection of family. The body had less energy and is turning inward to sustain the most important body functions for as long as possible. It is okay at this time to give the person "permission" to rest. Remember though not engaged in the conversation, the dying person's hearing remains very acute to the last breath. Hearing is the last sense to leave as the final sense of protection though the body is not able to respond.

With decreasing metabolism the dying person often experiences confusion and restlessness as the energy and life withdraws from the thinking part of the brain. The confusion usually is about who is there, visions and seeing loved ones who have already died. Approaching death sometimes is suddenly marked with a burst of energy and wakefulness where the dying person opens their eyes and is very clear with the persons with them. This is temporary. Loving, caressing and speaking words of release and comfort are very supportive at this time.

Restlessness and agitation appearing as repetitive motions such as pulling at the bed linens and clothing is due in part to metabolic changes and the decrease of oxygen to the brain. Understand that there is neither pain nor distress, rather a closing down of the body; it is not necessary to get in the way of the process.

Breathing
The drastic slowing of the breaths becomes noticeable with approaching death. The breaths become further apart and can vary in depth and regularity. This change from a normal breathing pattern usually marks the more imminent death. Gurgling sounds in the chest also known as "death rattle" may become very loud. This sound though distressful to the loved ones is from decreased fluid intake coupled with not being able to cough up the normal secretions. Family members often want the dying person to be suctioned as is may be interpreted as the person downing in their own fluids. In reality suctioning usually increases secretion and is discouraged.

There are three breathing patterns often seen as death becomes imminent. Cheyne – Stokes breathing is shallow breathing then no breathing for about 5 to 60 seconds. This breathing plus a similar one of periods of shallow panting – like breaths are related to diminished blood to internal organs. "Fish out of

water" breathing is labored breathing with gasping for air pro-
ducing an exaggerated gulping motion that appears to be grasp-
ing for air. These breaths become further and further apart until
they cease. The 'moment of death' exhale is an automatic reflex
exhale with no pain. It is the final release and letting go.

Blood pressure, pulse and circulation
Wide changes in blood pressure and pulse characterize the
last few days of life. The circulation withdrawing from the extremities into the inner organs can sometimes cause anger or
emotional outbursts such as anger and grief as the brain neu-
rons misfire. The dying person is usually not aware of them.

The temperature of the extremities begins to change from
very warm to very cold as the regulating mechanism begins
to weaken. Mottled or blotchy skin patches begin to appear
around the mouth, nose and extremities as well as on lower
body parts such as the back of the buttock, feet and legs. The
buttock blotchy skin is seen when the person is turned over
or onto the side. Skin colors begin to vary from rosy pink to
clammy to grey-blue or even purple.

As the circulatory system continues to fail, the blood pressure continues to become more erratic in volume, frequency
and intensity. With the failing of the last system, the circulatory system, death occurs.

Senses
Even the senses adapt, change and slowly diminish in the
last days. For smell there is a noticeable decrease in the

enjoyment of the aroma of foods, often with nausea or an upset stomach. A concomitant decrease in the taste of food is evident as the interest in food begins to wane. This is internally reflected as the body begins to shut down the digestive system. The sense of sight diminishes as seen in the eyes beginning to remain open with a glassy stare and inability to focus on outward objects. Sight is being withdrawn from the outer sensory world. Sometimes the dying person raises their hands up as if reaching for something. As the eyes become glassy and fixed, death is within hours. Hearing appears to be strong to the very end. Yet, the dying person cannot respond. Loving words and farewells are important at this time.

Imminent death
Imminent death can be within hours or minutes. It is often difficult to judge. Signs of imminent death include:

- Minimal speech
- Movement ceases
- Pulse weakens so it can be difficult to feel
- Blood pressure continues to drop
- Cheyne-Stokes respirations (slowing/pausing of breaths 5-60 seconds)
- Death Rattle ("gurgling" breathing sound)
- Pupils dilated and fixed (black center does not expand/contract to light)

Remember there is no pain; this is a normal natural process of closing down of all body functions.

The moment of death

Death comes unbidden without asking to everyone. To each it has to be entered alone. Loved ones and health professionals can only go to the edge. Death is a moment in time. The body knows how to create its self starting at the moment of creation; at the moment of death the body immediately begins to rapidly decompose/"uncreate" itself. The picture of death, the final closing down of all the body functions, looks something like this:

- The heart stops pumping
- Breathing comes to an end
- All muscles relax – urine/stool may be released
- The jaw usually opens slightly
- The eyes remain fixed and dilated

Summary

In the final days of life all systems of the body are systematically closing down. None are exempted. This process is natural, exquisite in its grand design, and experienced by everyone. Once we understand the process, death can begin to take its rightful place in physical life. It is one of the most important major events in every one's life second only to physical birth. Without death, life itself would have no conclusion, no culmination. To live forever would become a dread disease. But, death, itself, is not a disease to be treated and fought rather death is a normal natural process we can respond to with love, compassion, comfort measures and dignity. *Think about the body shutting down and consider how much better it could be in a lovely, peaceful Golden Room than in the usual acute care setting.*

Seven

After death rituals

Golden Room Options
Deciding on after death rituals

E ven *being in a place of gentle release at end of life we sometimes find that some of the after death rituals have not been finalized. The gentle caring atmosphere of The Golden Room may assists in calming the emotions and increasing the clarity around making these imminent decisions.*

These after death rituals are not necessarily related to the last few days. However, it is important to consider these ideas. It may be you, the family or close friend that makes some of these important decisions as your loved one spends their last days in The Golden Room.

For most people, just the thought of death is painful. To even begin to think about after death rituals is a step beyond what little comfort has been established so far in this book. Yet this is one of the most important and often overlooked parts of the dying process. What happens to the body? Can any of the final resting questions be taken care of ahead of time? As with any huge task we can break these down into smaller, more manageable pieces to deal with. And remember, it may feel like you are alone and your feelings are unique BUT, you are not. Help is at the tip of your fingers. This chapter is one of the first places to go.

Care of the Body: Who does what?
After the person has died, care, dignity and compassion do not stop. At each step health care professionals are mindful that a soul has just left this planet and their sacred task is to honor and respect the body. These are the assurances underlying how care after death usually occurs:

- Honoring the spiritual/cultural wishes of the deceased person and their family while making certain that legal obligations are met
- Respectfully preparing the body for transfer to mortuary, funeral home or the family
- Offering the family present the opportunity to participate in the care after death and supporting them to do so
- Ensuring the privacy and dignity of the deceased person
- Ensuring the health and safety of everyone coming in contact with the body
- Honoring people's wishes for organ and tissue donation
- Returning deceased person's personal possessions to their relatives

Who does what is the question that most people ask after the death of a loved one. To have some prior knowledge helps you to have a greater sense of control at a time when there is no control of the death that has just occurred.

There are many professionals involved in care after death including nurses, doctors, mortuary staff, hospital transport staff, ambulance staff, social services, funeral directors, bereavement counselors, and ministers/priests. Other professionals, depending on the type of death, may include coroners, pathologists, and police. Many of these professionals you will never see as they are behind the scenes, yet they are all important for things to run smoothly for you and your family.

For the purposes of this book we are looking at death that is expected and/or peaceful.

- At the time of death the physician on call or house nurse supervisor records the time of death, those present, the nature of the death and any important devices in use, signing their name and contact information in the appropriate record.
- The family may choose to sit with their relative immediately after the death allowing for last good byes or stay with them as part of religious customs or cultural/familial traditions.
- Family member may wish to assist with the personal care based on individual wishes, religious or cultural

requirements. Note the body changes can begin rather quickly after death which is a normal part of body decomposition.

- Personal care after death is the responsibility of the trained healthcare professional in hospitals, nursing homes, hospices or *Golden Rooms*.

Final Resting Preparations

<u>Who decides?</u>
You have control of your final resting preparations if you take that option. Here's the key: this is easiest done while you are healthy and before the end is near. At that time you can think clearly and can talk to as many people as necessary to get the message across. And it doesn't have to stop with talking about your preferences. You can make the calls and select just about everything in advance. This gives you time to look at costs and make wise choices. Last minute rushing because nothing was discussed beforehand often results in costing much more money. In order to do this, you need to think about what you would like, what others have done and what suits you. In short, this is your final farewell and you can do it your way.

<u>Looking your best</u>
Probably the last thing one thinks about in final resting preparations is looking your best. And yet, this is important as you won't have a mirror to look into before the big event. Women can probably relate to this more than men, but the fact still

remains that you want to look your best. How many times have you gone to a viewing and said or heard someone say, "Oh, she/he doesn't look like themselves." In order to look your best you need to have some photos available in which you do look your best – your hair, your coloring, your make up or lack thereof. These photos need to be known and accessible to your family so there is no last minute scramble to find the right picture.

Those of you that are opting for cremation or closed caskets do not have this option as your last viewing is usually at bedside while there is still some slight color in your checks and you are still warm. For a growing number of people this is becoming their choice. The reason for this is that they want to be remembered for who they were and how they loved others rather than what they looked like.

What to wear
Clothes that you look good in and what others think you look good in can be very different. We all have been in stores where the sales clerk has said how great we look in something that when we get home and try it on, it just doesn't look all that great. The same is true when the selection is made as to what to wear for your funeral. Choose something that you like that has colors that you usually wear. This is NOT the time to have on that funky outfit or suit that you are the only person who liked it or it is a color that you usually don't wear. This is the time to select what looks good on you. Remember that usually the top half is seen so shoes, socks even pants are not necessary.

Along with the perfect outfit also comes the question about jewelry. The same advice goes here also. Wear what you like. Often a wedding ring or favorite ring is on the hand. Be sure and let your family know that you want your jewelry removed and returned to the family after the viewing and before the interment.

Make a list of everything that you want to wear and were it is located. Keep this in a prominent place like in your dresser or in your jewelry box AND let your family know where it also is located.

Prepared / Prefunded arrangements

Prepared arrangements often called preplanning is becoming more and more popular. This involves selecting the funeral home and making the arrangements ahead of time. This is a tremendous gift to your family. There are three types of preplanning.

1. Wishes laid out: These arrangements are unfunded and on file with the funeral home, a family member or the executor for the estate.
2. Insurance funded policy: This policy is with a specific funeral home that guarantees and locks in the prices. It is easily transferable if you move out of the area. Usually you buy these from a national firm; local firms, if smart, will transfer them also. An insurance funded policy is the easiest for your family at the time of death. Payments can be made on a monthly basis and can start

at any age. It is best to check what is true for your state and locality.

3. A trust: This is bought from a funeral home with the money held in trust at a local bank. The money cannot be used until the time of death. Presently these are difficult to get since the money is not making much interest to help cover the increasing costs over time.

There are huge benefits to prepared/prefunding your final arrangements. More often than not, at end of life, most if not all of the financial resources have been used up with nursing homes, in home care and simply living longer than expected. This means there are little if any resources to pay for the final arrangements. People do not realize that the funeral costs must be paid in full before the funeral and disposition.

Within the family there are also huge benefits to prefunding besides the increasing cost. Adult children don't always get along, and at this time, often get highly emotional with different opinions of what to do with financial considerations. That bitterness and hurts can last for a long time. Although this is very real and should not happen, the family is all too often not on the same page at this time. Preplanning helps to eliminate some of this emotional and financial discomfort.

This prepared/prefunding is a type of celebration of your life which adds a gentle closure by:

• Relieving your family from stressful decisions
• Assuring your personal wishes

- Shelters funds if admitted to a nursing home
- Guarantees inflation proof funeral plans
- Gives you and your family peace of mind
- Allows you to select cremation, funeral plans, monuments
- Provides arrangements according to your wants and needs

Planning your own funeral

Can you imagine this actually being almost fun in a bitter sweet way? Think of this as planning a very important event in your life, which it is. The other most important event in your life was your birth. Now this is your moment, your last moment, and you can plan how you want it to be. Most people really don't like to think about their mortality much less plan for it. Planning your own funeral means realizing you are mortal and will one day die. It also means preparing for the inevitable. So why plan? For this very reason – no one knows when they will die. However, the likelihood grows larger the longer you live.

Planning can create a peace of mind not only for you but also your loved ones after you are gone. Planning now is a selfless act and a last gift to your loved ones that extends beyond your death.

There are eight areas of planning your funeral. Let's explore each one so you have a direction to move in and the basic information to get started.

1. What type of funeral?

There are actually seven types of common funerals. Surprised? You are probably only aware of a couple of them that are most common in your area. The funeral types look at how the body is prepared which is called a disposition.

<u>Traditional Burial</u> – This is the most familiar type of burial where the body is embalmed and casketed for burial in a cemetery.

<u>Cremation</u> – This is probably the second most common burial type where the majority of the body is literally "turned into light" by fire with some ash and bone fragments left.

<u>Green Funeral</u> – This funeral is about the chemical free preparation of the body which is casketed in either a cloth shroud or a biodegradable casket.

<u>Green Funeral and Green Burial</u> – This funeral incorporates the green funeral described above coupled with burial in a green cemetery in which no insecticides and pesticides are used.

<u>Home Funeral</u> – In this instance the family and friends lovingly wash and dress the body then place ice or dry ice beneath the deceased. In this way the body is preserved for about three days in which time the burial or cremation can take place.

<u>Burial at Sea</u> – In this instance the body wrapped in cloth or casketed is then released into the sea during a funeral service.

<u>Cryonic Preservation</u> – This is a controversial practice of preserving the body of the deceased who is legally dead through freezing.

2. Who needs to be notified?

- Family
- Spouse/ex-spouses
- Children/ grandchildren
- Parents
- Grandparents
- Brothers and sisters
- Other relatives
- Friends
- Neighbors and former neighbors
- Work colleagues
- Professional who have worked for you
- Spiritual leader – clergy, rabbi, priest, Imam
- Employer
- Insurance agent
- Lawyer
- Accountant
- Doctors
- Banker/financial advisor
- Creditors
- Organizations
- Social Security Administration
- Religious – church, temple, mosque
- Employment – current or former
- For military service contact Veterans Administration
- Places where volunteer time
- Clubs – hobbies, book, sports

- Alumnae organizations – high school, college
- Fraternal organizations
- Charities you support
- Political organizations

3. The actual funeral today may also be called a gathering or celebration of life.

There are many funeral styles to choose from – traditional formal services to destination funeral services. They can be combined in any way you desire. Choose what you are most comfortable with.

- A Living Funeral: This gathering is centered on someone who will die soon. Also known as End of Life Gatherings or Good bye parties they celebrate and honor the life that has been lived. Often times bon voyage or moving away cards are given with many well wishes.
- Traditional Funeral Service: This is a formal service with music, readings and a eulogy and/or inspirational message to pay tribute to the one who has passed and to give solace to the ones remaining behind. They usually occur within days of the death and prior to the burial. The location is either a place of worship or the funeral home.
- Visitation or Viewing: This is a time for the family and friends to gather with the casket open for a final acknowledgement and farewell.

- Home Funeral: This is a funeral held at a home usually a relative's. The friends and family act as the funeral director to wash and dress the body. Ice or dry ice is placed beneath the deceased out of view. The body lies in a bed or casket. The body can be kept this way for about three days. A home funeral allows family and friends an extended time for gathering, viewing, ceremonies/rituals and fellowship.
- Committal or Graveside Service: This service occurs at the place where the body will be buried or placed. Often this service is a extension of the service begun at the church/temple/funeral home. A committal or graveside service can also be the single and only service.
- Inurnment Service: This service accompanies the placement of the ashes into a permanent memorial site such as a mausoleum, a niche in a wall, columbarium, memorial garden, memorial ocean reef or other permanent site.
- Memorial Service: A Memorial Service is without the presence of the body and may be held weeks or even months after the death. It is often used to allow people from great distances time to plan and arrive to be part of the service. Cremation remains may be present.
- Scattering Service: A Scattering Service is a service that includes the actual scattering of the remains of the cremation usually in a select location that is meaningful to the deceased.

- Reception: The Reception often referred to as a wake is a gathering of friends and family. It may take place at the visitation or before or after the Service and involves food often brought in my family and friends.
- Family Gathering: A Gathering of people related to each other which may occur at anytime. Some families observe the anniversary of the loved one's passing. Others may observe the anniversary of the rebirth into spirit as part of their beliefs in the hereafter.
- Destination Funeral: This Service involves a group of family and friends who travel to a place of special meaning for an intimate memorial service.
- Direct: This involves a cremation or burial without any viewing or service.

After selecting the style of your funeral it is also important to select the tone for your funeral. This gives the organizers a definite guide to ensuring your last wishes. What would you like?

- Solemn and reverent
- Peaceful and reflective
- Joyful remembering
- Let it flow naturally
- Focus on this idea (be specific – positive memories, funny experiences, etc.)
- Doesn't make any difference

4. A Service and Reception Check list Ideas

The nice thing about planning ahead if you don't care, you don't have to choose, rather trust in your loved ones to make a great selection! This is really all about them and helping them to feel better and have one last memory.

<u>Who is in charge?</u> Choose a family member or loved one to work with the funeral director or another director so that the service runs smoothly. There are also funeral planning concierges and service event planners to assist in this process.

<u>Where is the service or reception to be held?</u>

- Funeral Home
- Place of worship – church, temple, mosque
- Outdoors – backyard, park, beach, or mountains
- Reception site – home, community center, restaurant, rented site
- Special significance location – theater, swimming pool, beach, library, golf course

<u>Who will officiate?</u>

- Loved one or friend
- Clergy
- Celebrant – someone legally authorized to conduct the service

Is there a tribute display? This is a collection of photos from your life and special objects of meaning in your life. With photos you might want to include date and location.

Do you want flowers? People often request no flowers rather donations to a special charity. Many people ask that they receive flowers now while they are alive so they can enjoy their scent and beauty. Again the choice is yours and yours alone.

- Easel display of wreath (everlasting life), heart or cross
- Flower spray on top of casket
- Flowers for grave side
- Flowers for around the urn
- Flowers for special people in your life
- Plant or season bulbs growing in pot for loved ones

Is there to be music and/or special songs?

- Write down your favorite songs to be sung
- Attendees to sing particular songs, hymns
- Recorded music on CDs
- Live music, jazz band, bagpipes, mandolin, string quartet

Are there to be readings at your service or gathering?

- Scriptures, poems, essays
- Who will read them?

- Do you want a eulogy? A eulogy is a talk or writing in honor of the deceased.
- Are there any specific things to include or exclude in the eulogy?
- Who would you like to deliver the eulogy?

<u>Are you a veteran and do you want to receive veteran's death benefits?</u> Veterans are eligible to receive burial at a national cemetery, a funeral flag, grave marker and other benefits.

- Do you want to be buried in a national cemetery?
- Do you want your family to receive a funeral flag?
- Do you want the funeral flag displayed at your funeral? Folded on top of the casket?
- Who do you want to keep the funeral flag?
- Do you want a funeral grave marker?
- Do you want a hearse at your funeral? A hearse is a commonly used vehicle to transport the casket or urn to the interment site. There are several different types.
- Traditional
- Motorcycle procession
- Horse drawn

5. Burial Details: What is your preference?

- Casket
- Viewing
- Pallbearer

- Burial site service
- Burial marker/ inscription/ made from
- Purchase grave liner

6. Cremation Details: What is your preference?

- View body before
- Keep remains to give to someone
- Store in urn
- Place in cemetery or columbarium niche
- Remains divided and given to different people
- Disperse remains in specific manner

7. My Obituary

- Do you want one?
- What would you like it to say?
- Who do you want named as survivors? This can be an issue in many families.
- Would you like memorial donations? If yes, name the recipient:

8. Other arrangements and last words

- Body/organ donor
- Paid for funeral package with funeral home/funeral concierge service
- Purchased cemetery plot

- Sample of DNA collected: Some states require DNA sample. The family pays for it.
- Like DNA collected before final disposition of body
- Final thoughts on my funeral and in general

Considering relatives

Ah yes, the relatives, they come in many shapes and sizes, opinions and life experiences. At this point in time, when the physical and spiritual worlds are very close and a reminder of their own mortality unconsciously rises to the unspoken surface, there can be many different thoughts and emotions emerging. Suffice it to say each one will handle their grief in their own way. Many cultures have special rituals to assist in this process and families are often closer during this time.

The legacy that you leave can be a great inspiration and comfort to your family and relatives. For the relatives left behind this is a time of remembering and allowing the sting of loss to gradually be replaced with cherish memories of joy… the memories of how the loved one lived rather than how they died.

Part Four
Before and After

The Tree of Life

The Tree of Life epitomizes
the natural cycle of life and death
through the seen and the unseen.

Eight

The first year after the
death of a loved one

Golden Room Options
Assisting the first year after death

E ven with a graceful, caring release from this life plane, the
first year after the death may still remain a challenge to
the loved ones. A good death greatly assists in this process
with a deep inner sense of gentle completion and release. This
death with dignity offers the loved ones a firm foundation to
begin the shift into life without the deceased. Though a bitter
sweet time, to have closure knowing that death was as gentle as
possible assists in the knowing that everything possible was done
to honor the loved one. Golden Rooms are being established to
support this process for everyone.

The first year of life after the death of a loved one is quite
possibly one of the most, if not the most, challenging life experiences. It is a period in which one has to adjust to new cir-
cumstances, a new living style both in his/her personal private
life and in their social life. Suddenly one is a widow and, like
it or not, that does separate you out from single or married.

With the loss of a parent, children also face a similar dilemma. Our culture does not speak to this. Rather the expectation after the funeral is to "get on with life." The first year becomes a monumental: "How can I ever live without...." Taking it one day at a time may sound cliché, but it really is the only way to approach this time. We all have a choice here. We can choose to either go through this adjustment period or we can grow through this time. "Going through" suggests resistance while "growing through" suggests an openness to discover and move through this time with as much grace and acceptance as possible.

Allowing the presence of grief
Everyone responds to loss of a loved one in their own way and in their own time. There is no magic bullet here. There are those time when one feels calm and peaceful, "in control" and "strong." There are other times when one feels sad and weepy. The swing in feelings is real and felt. The emotional work is to rebalance ourselves after the shock of the death – which death is – even when we know it is coming.

What we do know from personal experience and the experience of many others is that grief cannot be denied and nothing should stand in its way. In fact nothing does stand in grief's way as eventually if it is not expressed it comes out in other emotions such as anger, fear, aggression, depression, acting out, and increasing mood swings. If it is still not expressed it can lead to physical symptoms such as constipation, stiffness, allergies, shortness of breath, anxiety attacks.

We do know from experience is that as much as it appears to hurt, as hard as it seems to breathe, grief must be felt in order to be released. This is scary for many people. Yet, the rewards from sitting and honoring your grief is immense. Feel the feelings and allowing them to be. Watch your feelings as they change and shift. The feelings want to come up and be recognized. Allow them to be there and sit with them. They are spilling out and need to spill out. Sit with them again and again until the intensity begins to lessen. As it begins to lessen notice the subtle shift that is beginning to take place as you begin to step back and watch, rather than be consumed by grief.

As we become the watcher of our emotions rather than being lost in our emotions, we begin to discover a deeper peace, often call "the peace which passes all understanding," that begins to radiate from the empty inner space created by the loss. This peace begins to spread across our entire body and begins to fill us. This is often a gradual process. It's like the light of Eternal Love is beginning to fill us and we begin to turn to looking at this present moment rather than being lost in the past. Gradually there is an unconscious move towards a fulfilling life without a loved one. We find our self choosing life again.

This is not to say that we don't remember our loved one. We do. The pain of loss is gradually changed into cherishing the time we had together.

Letting go of tears and anger

Sometimes it can seem as if the tears will never stop; one will never stop hurting. We can be so consumed with the loss that life just does not seem possible. Some people spend lengths of time in bed or continually feel weak and helpless. The tears are your emotions' way of trying to adjust to the hole in the fabric of life that has been created. Anger is born out of frustration, the feeling of being helpless to stop death from happening. It is an inner anger and at times can be an anger aimed even at God. Letting go is actually a cleansing process that gradually begins to open us up to living in this moment.

The breath is our closest and constant companion and this is the time to use it and use it often. Simply focus on your breathing feeling the cool air going in and the warm air coming out. Keep focusing on the breath. You might even want to close your eyes or move into a soft gaze. This simple act allows the tears and anger to be come up without stopping or hindering them. It gives the body a mechanism to express the emotions. Sometimes you might forget to breathe with a wave of feelings, that's okay. Simply return to the breath when you remember. Time and practice make this an effective "habit" or response to tears and feeling that is a healthy letting go. Be gentle with yourself.

Giving away and reorganizing

Giving away and reorganizing takes many forms. With a home death the spouse or loved one who shared the bedroom needs to decide what to do. Some desire to immediate move the furniture around while others prefer to leave the bedroom just as it was. If there is a hospital bed and equipment many choose to remove these and put the room back as it was. Like with so many decisions in life there is no right or wrong decision. It is simply a choice that makes one more comfortable. This is difficult to know ahead of time.

Among the giving away and reorganizing there is another ritual of "last time." This is the realization of this is the last time I do something for the deceased person. These are often subtle yet each is a gentle realization that my life is different now and there is a gentle closing of the past. A woman called about a week after her husband's passing saying she finally did the washing. She paused then softly said, "This is the last time I can wash his clothes." With the realization comes another step in integrating the loss and bringing closure.

When it comes to giving away the deceased personal possessions this can take place quickly, done in degrees or over a longer period of time. Giving away the personal possessions like clothes, shoes, jewelry is healing as it is a signal that on some level the person is acknowledging the finality of the situation. Often the process begins with the more generic possessions and gradually moves into the more intimate and special meaning possessions like tickets to a special movie shared together or a special dress or aftershave. On the death of her father, one daughter wore his plaid winter jacket for the first winter as it brought her a feeling of comfort and reassurance that all was well. The second winter it was not needed and donated to a "winter coat for the cold" drive with the feeling that now it was time to have someone else enjoy the warmth that it offered.

Holiday Celebrations

Especially during the first year after the death of a loved one, holidays can be painful as memories arise about how it used to be and never be like that again. Seasonal holidays, birthdays, anniversaries, and family gatherings can be occasions to create rituals that are life enhancing, honoring the deceased while easing the pain of loss and surrounding feelings. For example, one widow chose to celebrate her husband's date of passing with a "Rebirth into Spirit" celebration complete with a re-birthday cake, a re-birthday song and a toast. The meal was filled with laughed as they chose to look at the great times and wisdom of their loved one. Another family spent their first Christmas without grandmother who had lived with them by taking a walk in the forest behind their home where she spend many hours in nature recalling her favorite stories about nature lore and watching for elves and woodland life. After unsuccessful cardiac resuscitation some hospitals have staff that encircles the bed for a moment of silence in honor of the one who has just passed into spirit.

Remembering

Remembering is another healthy aspect of life. We remember the good times and the bad. We remember things from our childhoods that are triggered by present events. This is also true of remembering our loved ones. This can be very healing. At first we are filled with memories of what it was like then and what it is like now – the loss, the hole that has been opened in our life. This is normal and natural. Over time our memories soften as the sting of loss begins to fade. When memories come up it might be a special food, a song, a place in nature or even a sunset. It can seem that the emotion is still raw. Stay with the emotion. Be the watcher of the emotion rather than becoming immersed in the emotion. Watch how the pain spreads to the cells of your body. Don't hold your breath with this process rather consciously breathe as you are the watcher. Trust that your breath and body know exactly what to do, which they do! As we let the emotion be expressed and dissipate, we make room for love and peace to emerge.

Maintaining hope and faith

Hope and faith come from things not seen and are what sustains us until we once again know and feel whole and safe. They come in many forms which often are not shared nor talked about to family and friends since they might be seen as odd or strange. One lady had a sense that her late husband was talking with her when she sat in his favorite chair so she got out a note book and asked him questions first about what to do and then more about what it was like where he was. She wrote everything down for many months. Then their daily times together became more erratic as she increasingly became involved with life again. Soon she talked with him when she just needed a little extra comfort. Ten years later she remembers how much that transition time was a time of comfort, hope and faith that she could go on without him.

It is not uncommon for people to talk with their loved one. After the death of his wife a Texas man would nightly walk the mile long road from his ranch to the highway and talk with her midst the starry night. On the walk out he talked; on the return walk he simply allowed himself to be connected with the immensity of the universe and could feel her love surround him.

Another woman upon the loss of her husband for many years would feel his warmth and presence as she fell asleep each night. And still another woman created a ritual of walking down to the lake like they did to watch the sunset and feel the connectedness with all nature. She would talk to the setting sun and feel connected to her husband and all of creation giving her insight, peace and wisdom.

Getting stuck and getting unstuck
For many people their grief has a gentle flow as loss turns into cherishing the time together. For others the loss seems to become built into the fabric of their personality and they don't know how to let it go… It has replaced the loved one and if they did let it go they would let go of their loved one and perhaps not be able to move on. This is a tough place to be in. Family may have been watching and wanting to help but feels a loss as to what to do. Asking for help from family, friends and even health professionals to get unstuck might be difficult, but it is usually beneficial. It is possible to let go of the hurt, cherish our loved one in our heart and live a full life again.

After the first year of loss of a loved one the anniversary dates still are remembered yet there is the beginning of a softening of the feeling around the loss. The person is never lost or forgotten, they are always within our heart. Even years later, a song or a picture can evoke a sentimental soft response of remembering and cherishing.

The first year rituals after the loss of a loved one are in many ways a rite of passage in order to go on with your life and find meaning. These gentle closures pave the way for a gentle reentry into moving on with your life.

Nine

Getting Ready

Golden Room Option
Getting Ready for the Golden Room

A t the end of life everything seems to be happening in the present moment since all thoughts are focused on the moment at hand and one is alert and aware. *Thinking about the past or what one needs to do outside of this moment is relatively brief. In what appears to be a relatively short amount of time there is a building to a climax at the moment of death. Living in this moment today, right now, means accepting life on life's terms and learning to respond gently in each moment rather than becoming angry or frustrated. We might not be able to change what is happening but we can control the quality of the experience. Life is about living and enjoying each moment and feeling everything and being okay with those feeling – the comfortable and the uncomfortable.*

The actual dying process usually commences well before the physical death and is a personal journey. As with any journey there is a process of getting ready. With death this is a gradual often unconscious preparation of making slight adjustments to our day or the way we do things.

One of the first things many people notice is having to hold the book or reading source a little further away from their eyes. The computer screen may become difficult to read and we discover how to increase the font size and/or the size of the entire page. Some of us stop at the drug store and look for magnifying glasses while others have their eyes checked and start to wear prescription glasses. Many laugh about needing glasses when they first put them on in public yet soon take their glasses for granted.

We automatically begin to make small adjustments to our balance, our bending and stooping, our lifting and carrying, the speed we move through our day, the volume of the television or you tubes, walking up and downstairs, modify our exercise routine or intensity and many more activities of daily living.

Currently there is no consensus on when end of life begins. Often a sudden change in health or wellbeing is noticeable. The actual dying process can take many years before it is completed. Since no one knows the exact time of death or the length of dying, slowing down may actually be the beginning of the end. Often this is seen in older people as they become less flexible and less mobile. The muscle mass especially in their shoulders begins to decrease. When hugged they feel frail through visually they do not appear frail. Their diet changes to softer, more easily digested foods. Often times these are processed convenience foods. Thirst mechanisms diminish and less water is consumed while the increasing concern is being able to get to the toilet on time. Days become constricted to getting up, dressing, breakfast, dishes, maybe one small activity then lunch, dishes, perhaps a nap and/or small activity, supper, dishes and an earlier and earlier bedtime. As this cycle repeats there is a growing awareness that not much is being accomplished during the day. It is taking all their energy for activities of daily living.

A physical distancing from the world outside the immediate becomes more and more noticeable. The person's interests and range of activity becomes progressively smaller. Often long trips are no longer taken or the spontaneity of doing something is declined. Driving slowly changes with the decrease in physical activity and gradually becomes only to the grocery store or around town and during the day light. Other arrangements are made for needed things which are often brought to the person by family and friends. This gradual distancing from the world also includes getting one's affairs in order. There seems to be an inner knowing that the time on earth is short and plans need to be made to exit.

Graceful aging all along the way
Healthier lifestyles research suggests that about 30 more years can be added to the life span. It is never too late to start a healthier life style through results may vary. One thing is for sure: to gracefully move through life is life enhancing and results in a positive attitude and often a zest for living. A sense of self humor greatly aids the aging process.

Whatever the age to live gracefully is to accept the aging process yet, modify the things that we can modify. We also need understanding to know the difference between what we must accept and what we can modify. Graceful aging is enhanced through gratitude. It's being able to let go of what we were able to do or accomplish in the past and be thankful for what we are able to accomplish today. It is to be able to smile when we are tired and allow our body the time to rest and replenish. It is being able to ask for help in a kind loving way and to accept help in a kind loving way. It is in knowing that many things do not need to be done immediately and can wait. It is being okay where we are, who we are and what we are. Graceful aging is allowing life to move at its own pace rather than pushing and pulling to get the last ounce out of the day or our body. Graceful aging is enjoying ourselves, our children, our grandchildren and our friends at whatever age they are at.

About 30 years ago there was a study that questioned society's beliefs about older people and their potential. A select group of seniors were taught breathing exercises, meditation, deep relaxation, yoga, biofeedback plus techniques to expand their creativity and use more of their brain through art, music, movement, and group discussions. The seniors found a new lease on life as they refined their "declining years" into healthy life styles through practical ways to cope with personal challenges along with a healthy self-image.

We all have been young; we all will grow old. Where ever we find our self is just the perfect place to be and rejoice because that is where we are. To paraphrase May West, the popular goddess of vaudeville, it's not the years in your life; it's the life in your years!

The art of reminiscing

There is a real art to reminiscing! This is a natural process of describing past events and adventures either to ourselves or family and friends. Many people keep personal journals or write annual holiday letters to share their lives with others. Think of how much time you talk about your plans, goals, abilities, successes, letdowns and failures. These are all forms of reminiscing which mainly focus on the immediate past. Today in many circles they would be called "my story" or "drama." Many people spend the larger part of the day telling others about their life as if to say, see how important I am and how important my life is.

There is another part of reminiscing; it is the remembering of childhood, schooling, your parents, your aspirations, your hopes and dreams. This reflection contains a deeper understanding of how one's life has unfolded. It's seeing the patterns, twists and turns that have brought you to this point in time. It is about being with the memories and seeing them for what they are – memories – and not getting caught up in the emotions surrounding them. Rather there is a gentle smile of realization of that was then and this is now. Both are good and both have elements of love and disappointment.

Reminiscing is about separating out the past from the present and living at this point in time. When we live in the past we are unable to embrace life and all it has for us in this moment.

The natural process and evolution

There is a natural process and evolution that we continue to move through as we are born, grow up, live our lives, and eventually die. The physical process is the one most familiar to us. The mental/psychological and spiritual are other processes that aren't as well known or talked about. It is good to briefly look at them as they all blend together to shape and form who we are and how we approach death and dying. They all participate in getting ready to die.

Mental/Psychological Evolution

Our mental/psychological development begins on the day of our birth and continues our entire life. Our early experiences before we have words color our experiences throughout our entire life. Without words these early experiences are stored as emotions that act as guides to what we need to do in our life to be loved and feel safe. As strange as this may seem to read, more and more evidence is being uncovered to support this strong effect of our learning before we understood words. This does not mean that we are helpless or can justify our actions or words by saying, "Well, that is just how I've been wired." Rather this is our cutting edge where we need to begin to take responsibility for our words and actions and take the time to go deeper into their inner cause.

We have been taught that we react to our environment. This is only partly true. In reality we react to our present environment based on our past experiences that go way back to those first months of life. It is all about feeling loved and what we have to do to gain approval again. If we learned that we need to feel afraid and cry loudly to be loved, then those are the emotions that surface now. The expression of those emotions takes different forms over the years. Feeling afraid might first be expressed by crying loudly then changes as an adult into shouting when we are afraid or bursting into tears. We all have seen a TV program or movie that causes us to become tearful, fearful or loving. The movie has stimulated an emotion from our past. When we critique the movie, we say we liked it or that's not for me. These critiques are based on our past experiences and have nothing to do with the movie or TV program. Essentially, our past conditioning from our family, culture, and society has determined how we respond in the present moment. This is a very simplified explanation of the process.

Spiritual Evolution
Stories and Beliefs
Our beliefs and values based on our stories are the foundation we have built that reinforces our life's journey; they help us find meaning and purpose in our life. They build hope and reinforce the need to take many small steps towards our goals and aspirations. They show how we have put effort into our lives in order to achieve a goal. They can reinforce our desire to

keep moving forward. Our stories serve as bench marks along the way to help us recognize our choices, successes, strengths, areas to improve and refine our goals. Our stories provide a feeling of connection with ourselves, others and life itself.

For some people their stories and beliefs actually hold them back. Too many times they are looked upon as things lost and never to be replaced again… senior year in high school…being on a sport's team…their first love….their perfect birthday…. their one day of fame. Sorry to say, this is an error of thinking that actually prevents us from moving forward and enjoying life in this moment. It's like we become stagnated at a point in time and refuse to acknowledge the fact that we are growing older, times change, situations change. We have a choice to use our stories and beliefs as building blocks to move us forward or to use them to keep us from moving forward – like life has passed us by. It is often at this place where we become second hand people in that we live vicariously through the lives of our grandchildren, our children, movie stars or people we highly respect. To regain ourselves and move forward means that we recognize that life is lived in this moment. The past is a memory and no longer real. It is never too late to have a happy and fulfilled life.

Learning forgiveness
One of the gentle things that often occurs as we grow older is forgiveness. Learning forgiveness might be an unconscious realization of aging. Perhaps life has taught us that forgiving takes a lot less energy. Maybe forgiving is a learned experience.

Certainly, forgiveness is essential to a full rich life and peaceful death.

Feeling guilty of past actions or assigning blame often results in depression and or anger. Both of these emotions are very destructive to the body, color our feelings about other things and rob us of the energy to enjoy life. These negative feelings silently deprive us of not only energy but time, precious time, in creating loving relationships and focusing on end of life aspirations ... our goals and "bucket list."

As we begin to forgive our self, then we are able to forgive others. Both can be challenging; both are necessary. Forgiving begins by letting go of the self-blame for past actions. The underlying ability to forgiving our self is to become really honest with our self as to what worked or didn't work in our life. Living our life from a place of forgiveness, we find our self in a new space of increasing unconditional love. We begin to ask our self "how can I criticize another while expecting others to accept where I am?" With living the answer to this question we begin to experience more love, peace, abundance and joy. These are the gifts of unconditional love that are given as we keep releasing and letting go of anything and everything that causes us even a moment of hesitation, fear, anger or resentment. These are gifts of forgiveness.

Becoming Peaceful

Becoming peaceful is not something that we suddenly wake up with in the morning. Rather it is something that we have to practice in each situation that comes up in our life.

119

Praying for peace often results in what appears to be an up-surge in stressful situations in order for us to learn being peaceful. Becoming peaceful is part and parcel a gift of our unconditional loving. As such the only place we can express unconditional love is in the present moment. What this means is we need to practice living more in the present moment. In fact we often get into trouble when we talk and/or think about the past and pass judgments on what happened or didn't happen.

Relaxation and meditation are excellent ways to become peaceful and increasingly be in the present moment. We can only relax or meditate in the present moment. One way that many people discover to help stay in the present moment is through the power of their breath. Think about it. Your breath is always with you so it is accessible. You are already breathing so there is nothing you need to add or learn. It is unnoticeable to other people so you can focus on your breathing any place even during a conversation. Our brain can only focus on one thing at a time so when we are focusing on our breathing and feeling the air going in and out, our mind cannot think about the past or the future. AND, we can breathe and listen to a conversation or observe what is going on around us. Listening and observing from this moment means that our responses can come from a very clear place inside rather than from a fearful, blaming mind. What have you got to lose? Try it. The three things that are required to be success with the breath keeping you in the present moment are: practice, practice, practice.

Grief and loss

Grief and loss is usually associated with end of life and with the loved ones left behind. In actuality grief and loss happens on a regular basis all through our lives and also involves the dying person as they review their life. Grief is a necessary part of the dying process for all those involved whether directly or indirectly. Usually the closer the relationship with the deceased, the stronger the grief response. In turn this affects every part of one's life… our health, emotions, relationships, spirituality, meaning of life and even to taking care of ourselves.

The dying person integrates the increasing physician visits, the tests and therapies which becomes the main focus of their life. As the news of deteriorating health spreads, visits from family and friends increase and they are welcome. At the same time there is a gradual withdrawing of the dying person from the outer activities as they become more reflective and inner focused.

A change is felt in the dying person where their thoughts and activities become more and more immediate. They seem to redefine many of their hopes and dreams to be immediate rather than long term such as the shift from recovery to relief of pain. Hope is a little better than despair. It's staying slightly positive in an inevitable situation. And, in and of itself has a calming effect on both the physical body and the emotions. The dying person is often of comfort to those around them.

One's spiritual practices become of greater assistance for the dying person as they move into a place of acceptance of the inevitable. Many people discover that when the veil between the physical and spiritual world thins at the end of life they can find comfort and assurance even if they have not had a "spiritual/aware" life. Consider the fact that living in the present moment is literally forced upon all of us at end of life as our body closes down and prepares for the inevitable. We can choose to accept what we cannot not change, the dying process, and move into a place of grace and tenderness that assists a gentle release or go kicking and resisting. We always have a choice. Choose wisely.

Transcendence
Transcendence feels like a very spiritual word which simply means to rise above or go beyond. In self transcendence there is a going beyond time such that the feeling of past and future recede into the background as a foundation for the present moment. As we move beyond our self in the present moment we can discover service to other people and also towards meaning in our life. Transcendence takes many forms such as through the family, work, creativity, through being receptive and understanding of others and where they are or accepting things that cannot be changed. With death it is actually transcending death into the greater understanding of the eternal cycle of life and balance. This transcendence is heard in gospel songs as "death where is thy victory; death where is thy sting."

At end of life transcendence is lived in the present moment without regret, neglect nor hopelessness, rather a sense of one moment in time then another moment in time with death being simply a moment in time and a natural part of the life cycle.

Stop here and reflect on what you just read and sense how comfortable or not you are with this thought. Our senses give us pointers to places in our life where we need to spend time and become comfortable with things we cannot change rather than sweep them under the carpet. As we reflect on our lives now and through our life time we can begin to find meaning and connectedness. This in turn increases our transcendence and feeling of peace.

Often times a life review or story of this life, brings meaning. Remembering those who we love and discovering one's place in history brings a sense of peace and closure. Each life is important; each life has added a depth and quality to this planet. No other life would have done this in the same way. No life is any more important than another. Each life is deserving of peace, rest and dignity.

Nearing death awareness

Nearing death awareness occurs in the final stages of dying as the person is aware that they are nearing death. They often talk about what they are experiencing and frequently request something that needs to be completed for a peaceful death. (NOTE: This is not a near death experience which occurs as a result of a heart attack, trauma or drowning where a person is aware of leaving their body and quickly returning.) Often the person drifts between the dimension that lies beyond them and the physical dimension. This could be considered another form of transcendence that one comes in and out of. This slower dying process permits time to evaluate one's life and what needs to be finished before death. Those ready to leave often have a look of peace and understanding on their face. They can offer a gentle reassuring touch to others. Their sense of knowing and acceptance is palpable.

Getting ready to die is a personal journey that everyone takes with no exceptions. It offers the opportunity for closure on many levels as well as assisting our loved ones to accept and begin their closure which will continue after our demise. Just as our body will be closing down this period is also a time when our life is coming to a close with a final review and release.

Each life is important. It's not how much we have accomplished on the outside rather this is the time that we complete our inner work of loving, giving our final gifts of peace and understanding and moving into releasing ourselves to the ever nearing end of life as we have known it.

Additional considerations
Consider 611

Remember back in chapter 1 when we discussed what happens when a person calls 911? Here is the flip side of that which is just now coming into focus. What if, and this is a big if, at the end of life instead of making a call for emergency aid and transport to an emergency room (ER or ED) one could call 611. This would be a call to receive comfort and assistance in recognizing the normal end of life process. Rather than being sent to a traditional ER or ED setting designed to save lives, you would be given instructions on how to go to a *Golden Room* or *Golden Room Center*. The 611 would be a system to assist you to avoid all the needless emergency care and move more easily into a natural end of life. In other words, the 611 centers would have trained responders to help you identify and allow the natural process. **THIS IS ONLY AN IDEA AT THIS TIME,** but one to consider and imagine with us how to implement and make it a reality.

Consider Cell phone stand-by help
Until we have a 611 phone system, there is another option. Buy a cell phone for the person at end of life. Low cost, with prepaid minutes cell phones are available at retail outlets such as Wall Mart or K Mart. Program in at least three phone numbers of nearby family, caregivers, or friends who could immediately respond to the person in distress. Work out and practice a scenario that reassures the person using the phone that their contact persons will answer the phone and will immediately come to them in a time of acute distress. This adds an important layer of comfort to the end of life person and will serve to allay their fright if and when the time comes that they may actually need to use their phone to summon help.

The people on the dial up list need to understand that the call is for comfort, palliative end of life care and not a call to ask for emergency medical service. They too must be a part of the end of life support system.

It is important to consider both what is and what could be as we prepare to die. These examples given above are a few of the possibilities. Many more will come forward as we prepare for end of life both personally and as a nation of compassionate people who are beginning to wake up to the need for high quality end of life care.

Part Five
Completing these thoughts

The Tree of Life

The Tree of life embodies your natural cycle of blending thought, facts, options, and unique physicality with the emotional, inner foundation, and unseen into actions.

Ten

Now what?

Golden Room Option
Next steps

We all are learners and we all are teachers. What we learn we can pass along to others to assist them in their journey. Certainly one place we can do a lot of teaching is with our physicians. Many of us already do this as we share our supplements or something we have read or are trying to decrease our pain or increase our mobility. So what you can do is to begin to educate your physicians about Golden Rooms? Write down and give them the website: www.GoldenRoomAdvocates.org As with anything the more a topic is talked about and shared the more power and awareness it generates. As we share Golden Room information there can be both a giant ground swell that stimulates a change in the health care profession and how we view death and dying. And it all starts with small steps. Talk to your physician, your nurse. Ask if they have heard about Golden Rooms. Ask and keep asking and eventually they will become curious and begin to search out information. One small step becomes one giant leap for death with dignity.

We've come to the last chapter and hopefully we have given you practical guidance and information. Our attempt was to lay out the facts as clearly and concisely as possible. To offer you resources that will be helpful and give you a greater sense of knowing what to expect. A lot of what will happen to you is an individual experience depending on you, your attitude, outlook on life, your family, your preparations, your physician and nurses.

Your choices
Human nature being what it is, we love to have choices rather than being told what to do. You actually have three choices on how to proceed.

First, having finished this book tell your friends or your book club how wonderful it was and how it explained so much to you. You might even share with them some of your discoveries. Knowledge is an interesting thing; once you have it, it is great to be able to use it.

The second choice is to put it down and do nothing. Do not share it nor begin to prepare for your eventual death. This accomplishes nothing for you. If this is fear or a sense of an impossible task that you choose to do nothing, please go back and reread some of the chapters. Or you can visit www.goldenroomadvocates.org and look at the beautiful pictures and feel the gentle calmness that enfolds you. Or you can begin to use the breathing technique to assist you through the fear as we described earlier. You really do have many choices. Doing nothing is really not the best choice.

The third choice is to begin to take action on the things that you do have control over and there are plenty. Start by breaking things down into doable pieces. Do the easy ones first. If you need assistance with this, ask a family member or friend. Let others be involved in your process. Talk about it and share your progress.

Taking action involves accepting responsibility for what is going to happen and developing a guide to assist others in carrying out your wishes. This action is relatively easy for you because you have most of the information at your finger tips. Your family does not have this intimate detail of your finances, your wishes or even the simple information of your email address and access code. Imagine the frustration and helplessness that can be avoided simply by you taking the time to sit down and collect this information all in one place.

There is an old adage that says "you can take a horse to water but you can't make it drink." I would add "but you can make sure the horse is thirsty when it gets there." By the very fact that you have purchased this book is an indication that you are thirsty for this information. And, having completed this book you are now ready to begin an action plan to actually do the work that is need.

Review the information that is needed. Divide the information into small sections so you can see progress. Begin to fill in the blanks. Put all the sections together. Date the finished copy. Print several copies. Decide where to have your master copy. Tell your family/friends where it is located. Give them each a copy. Decide on a yearly date to review the information. Put the date on your calendar. Smile on a job well done.

One way to keep yourself on track is to do this together with a friend or family member. To have a buddy who is also collecting their information and making end of life decisions really helps to keep you on track and not lose your momentum. Being able to talk over the ideas and preferences will certainly assist you in making your decisions.

A gift in your hands

There is no challenge without a gift in its hand. We have the challenge because we need the gift. The challenge here is at the end of your physical life to move through this process with as much dignity and grace as possible surrounded with loving, kind people in an atmosphere that supports everyone. Any gift, in order to be appreciated, must be used. We must meet the challenge, take small steps and accomplish our task. The gift is the dignity and love that we all crave our entire life. We are bringing that into being now for ourselves and our loved ones through our actions.

We know that the steps outlined seem like a lot. We both have been through this and are finding new things to consider and ways to make it simple. This is the gift of this book that we are passing on to you.

Our passion and our desire is to have, within the next generation, a realization of death with dignity for all through *Golden Rooms* to the point that everyone will say:

"How did we ever live or peacefully die without
Golden Rooms?

The Tree of Life

www.GoldenRoomAdvocates.org

NOTES

NOTES continued

PEOPLE TO NOTIFY

PEOPLE TO NOTIFY continued

QUESTIONS TO ASK

QUESTIONS TO ASK continued

INFORMATION TO FIND

INFORMATION TO FIND continued

Made in the USA
Lexington, KY
11 May 2018